PERFORMANCE ANALYSIS AND APPRAISAL:

A How-To-Do-It Manual for Librarians

ROBERT D. STUEART
MAUREEN SULLIVAN

HOW-TO-DO-IT MANUALS
FOR LIBRARIES
Number 14

Series Editor: Bill Katz

NEAL-SCHUMAN PUBLISHERS, INC.
New York, London

Published by Neal-Schuman Publishers, Inc.
100 Varick Street
New York, NY 10013

Printed and bound in the United States of America

Library of Congress Cataloging-in-Publication Data

Stueart, Robert D.
     Performance analysis and appraisal : a how-to-do-it manual for
 librarians / Robert D. Stueart, Maureen Sullivan.
         p. cm.—(How-to-do-it manuals for libraries ; no. 14)
     Includes bibliographical references and index.
     ISBN 1-55570-061-6
     1. Librarians—Rating of—Handbooks, manuals, etc.   2. Librarians—
 Job descriptions—Handbooks, manuals, etc.   3. Library personnel
 management—Handbooks, manuals, etc.   4. Library employees—Job
 descriptions—Handbooks, manuals, etc.   5. Library employees—Rating
 of—Handbooks, manuals, etc.   I. Sullivan, Maureen.   II. Title.
 III. Series.
 Z682.28.S88   1991
 021'.9—dc20   91-17288
                                                          CIP

TO MARLIES AND JACK
FOR THEIR FAITH, LOVE, AND ENCOURAGEMENT

CONTENTS

LIST OF FIGURES

PREFACE

Performance Analysis and Appraisal is a basic how-to-do-it guide intended to answer important questions about the use of the library's most vital resource, its staff. Our discussion is set in the context of other human resource management issues. These issues are presented as a simple exploration of how the individual person may be productively integrated into the goal of successful library and information services.

We ask you such questions as: Does your library or information system have a human resource development program? How is it determined? What personnel resources are needed? How does it achieve success in this quest? Does the organization actually need or even really want a total human "systems" process that begins with a careful look at the job, how individuals are recruited, and how they are evaluated and encouraged to grow on the job? Are there advantages to such a plan? Conversely, what are the pitfalls in trying to introduce one? How do you go about designing a job and then hiring the right person to fill it? Are there any really effective evaluation processes and, if so, how can they be applied in a particular library? Just as important, how can you implement and evaluate such a process? We then go on to help you answer these questions.

A plethora of books and articles in the management literature deal with the challenges of describing jobs, interviewing potential employees, and, reviewing and evaluating the performance of individuals working in organizations. Surprisingly, comparatively little exists about practices and processes in libraries and other information centers. This volume is intended to fill part of that void to help both supervisors and staff understand the positive outcomes which can be achieved through a well-constructed, fairly administered process for the evaluation of the performance of individuals working in libraries.

It is an oversimplification, perhaps even a cliche, to say that people are the key to the effective functioning of labor-intensive organizations such as libraries and other information centers. To further develop that resource, people working in organizations must be told in straightforward language what is expected of them and how well they are performing to meet those expectations. The supervisors also must know how to conduct such a process successfully. Therein lies the challenge—to enable employees to understand this process and their individual accountability for achieving both individual and organizational objectives. As a motivator, people working in organizations need to be told that they are doing a good job or that their actions need improvement. "How am I doing?" is in the mind if not on the lips of every employee. Success in stating the parameters and then measuring performance is important to the individual and the organization.

Three of the most important components, the key ones, in human resource development are the description and analysis of jobs in the organization; the recruitment and introduction of the best individuals into the library's work environment; and finally the performance evaluation and assessment of individuals filling the positions. Those components are interrelated and form the central core of any development program. They are the focus of *Performance Analysis and Appraisal*, which is supplemented with examples of forms, policies and processes located in the appendixes. These are intended as examples only and are not necessarily suggested as models, although most are very good examples.

ACKNOWLEDGMENTS

The authors wish to thank Pat Schuman, President of Neal-Schuman Publishers, for her gentle encouragement to undertake this writing, and Nancy Viggiano and Susan Holt at Neal-Schuman for their persistence in bringing it to fruition. Thanks are also due to Margaret Myers, Director of ALA's Office for Library Personnel Resources for her advice.

INTRODUCTION

Human resource management, the current vogue term for staff recruitment, utilization, evaluation, and development, focuses attention on the most valuable assets that a library organization can employ to meet its service objectives. *Human resource management* evolved from earlier concepts of manpower planning and personnel utilization. The emphasis, changed over the years, is now upon the employee as an asset rather than a cost factor and upon long-term development and retention of employees rather than short-term benefits to meet current conditions. Analyzing human resource needs and developing programs, and policies to satisfy them is becoming more necessary in libraries. Role identification and change, influenced by technology on the one hand and economic constraints on the other, require the library organization to demonstrate its accountability in many ways. One of the most important is through the effective assessment and utilization of personnel. Legislation governing the hiring, firing, and dismissal of employees has reduced flexibility even as personnel costs have accelerated. Issues of equal pay for equal work and comparable worth also require a commitment to the process of evaluation and reward.

Effective utilization of human resources in such a dynamic setting is imperative to meet the library's goals, as well as to motivate each staff member by instilling a sense of self-worth and contribution. Research has shown that employee satisfaction and productivity are greatest when individuals perceive that their own personal and professional goals are compatible with the objectives of the organization. Performance evaluation of, and feedback to, individuals working in libraries and other information centers under such circumstances has become a necessary and continuous process.

Under such conditions, it is surprising how many organizations resist the need to develop formalized processes. It is also naive not to recognize that when one person is working under the direction of another in an organization, there is likely to be an evaluation process in place, whether it is informal and subjective, or formal and more objective. It is also less than beneficial to hurriedly describe a position vacancy when that vacancy occurs without previous reflective analysis of what is needed. In too many instances, if the informal process is in effect, the position description is based on intuition, impression, inuendo, and/or intolerance. In an ideal setting, those factors can be anticipated, since people act or in many cases react to the body language, attitudes, values, personalities, ethnic backgrounds, experiences, physical presence, and similar characteristics of the persons with whom they are involved in a work situation. In selecting new staff members or evaluating current ones, reactions often are based upon the opinion holder's own individual priorities, biases, mores, expectations, and values. Sometimes competition or envy influence those relationships. Coworkers being evaluated sometimes experience covert peer pressure which forces conformity to a performance norm, or potential employees are rejected because they do not meet a subjectively developed mold.

If the evaluator is also the supervisor, other dynamics affect the process and monetary reward can become an overbearing consideration, particularly if the performance evaluation is perceived as being connected to a salary review. In the management literature there is an ongoing debate about the value of both peer review and linking an appraisal process, formalized or not, to merit salary adjustments. The debate, by extension, relates to the hiring, promotion, transfer, and termination process as well.

Libraries are being challenged to be accountable for their actions and much attention is being focused on developing performance and output measures for most kinds of libraries—academic, public, school, and special. Those documents, guidelines, and standards address the need to effectively utilize human resources in meeting goals set out in a formal service plan.

The need to understand each person's role, how that role is translated into a job designation, how it relates to the goals of the larger organization of which it is a part, how the individual is or should be recruited, and how that individual's performance is evaluated by the organization is critical in that accountability. Role definition seems to be one of the most difficult objectives to accomplish. Role clarity is the degree of congruence between the perceptions of the employer and the employee about the latter's role which then sets the parameters for effective job performance and measurement of that performance.

Not only does such a process reveal how successfully an individual is contributing to organizational goals, it also addresses the quality of work life and can minimize work stress by revealing to the employee how well he or she is performing. Understanding this factor has the potential for increasing job satisfaction, decreasing anxiety, and improving self-esteem. A process that recognizes the strengths and weaknesses of employees and promotes improvement in job performance also promotes self-confidence and motivation. This formalized communication process, then, can be the key to the development of employees as individual workers and as team players in the organization.

In effective human resource utilization several objectives can be identified for a formal plan. First, the organization must know what is wanted and needed to fulfill service goals. This can be determined by analyzing work requirements, developing job specifications, and preparing the necessary policies and procedures to hire personnel. Following that, the primary aim is to recruit and retain the best qualified and most productive staff for the library organization. Both aspects play a key role in the evaluation process.

Once an individual has been recruited, the best use should be made of that employee's talents, skills, and abilities so that satisfaction and development can be encouraged. Previously, many libraries relied heavily upon longevity rather than performance as a guide for advancement. When longevity resulted in automatic promotion into supervisory positions without demonstrated competence, the "Peter Principle" (good individuals being promoted into positions beyond their capabilities) could be observed in action. This has now changed.

Another important factor is for the organization to be able to anticipate effective human resource utilization by identifying strengths and weaknesses in the total personnel pool and to take positive staff development actions to correct behavior on the one hand or reward behavior on the other.

Finally, it is important to tie the human resources plan of strategy for the library to the mission and resources of the larger organization, whether that is an institution of higher education, a for-profit company, a school district, or a city or town government.

Some libraries have created personnel departments and assigned specific staff to the mechanics of a personnel system. In addition to factors already mentioned, the personnel department normally oversees wages, salary and other benefits, health and safety issues, etc. Even in those situations, responsibility for the development of staff and the pursuant review process rests primarily with the individual line supervisor through interaction with each individual employee. It is usually the manager of a department, unit, or function who is primarily responsible for describing the job, analyzing it, recruiting the right person, and evaluating the performance of the individual occupying that position. Those supervisors are the ones most responsible for identifying significant changes as they occur in the workplace and suggesting alternatives or adjustments to meet changing conditions. However, it is the responsibility of the human resources staff to develop, revise, and maintain job descriptions, and to develop policies and procedures for that review and evaluation. Such centralization ensures that there is consistency and that standardized procedures are followed. In a smaller organization, with no specific human resources staff, this may mean the centralization effort is developed through the director's office. In any case, it is a continuous, interactive process.

To give the human resource utilization process objectivity, substance, and meaning; to encourage individuals to grow in their current positions and aim for promotion to more challenging ones; to place performance in proper perspective within the goals of the library; and to address both ethical and legal questions, a formal description and evaluation of performance is necessary. Implementation of such a formal process requires careful planning to avoid costly mistakes and threatening procedures. To minimize resistance and resentment among staff, all individuals who will be affected should be involved: supervisors and supervisees, from library pages and student assistants, through volunteers, support staff and professionals all the way up to the director and other management staff.

Overcoming the stress created by uncertainty is the greatest challenge to initiating a new system. Supervisors will need help in analyzing positions and developing job descriptions. They are likely to be hesitant at first to point out negative aspects of performance and can experience real difficulty in removing subjective aspects from the process once it is established. At the same time, those being evaluated may perceive a challenge to their esteem and self-worth, as well as a questioning of their abilities. Those challenges can be overcome through an educational process with open channels of communications. A careful explanation of why, how, and when should precede any change to the current arrangements. This should begin with an overall review of the different jobs in the organization with the people who are currently occupying those positions. The next chapters address the most important aspects of that human resources development process.

THE JOB

Jobs are the individual pieces from which an organization is created and derives its potential for growth. New jobs are created and existing ones are enhanced or eliminated when the overall objectives of the organization become too large or complex for the current work force, or shift in a different direction. By first describing jobs and then positioning them together on the basis of similarity and relationships, the organization can more effectively function as one unit with a stated mission. Within libraries there are several groups of jobs: those held by volunteers, hourly employees, support staff—including paraprofessionals and clerical employees—maintenance and security personnel; and those held by other salaried employees, primarily professionals in both the librarian category and other specialists such as the budget officer and archivist.

CREATION

In considering the creation or further development of a job, it must first be placed into the context of the changing work environment which perpetuates a constant shifting of how jobs relate to each other within the organization. The behavioral context in which jobs exist affects the performance of each person in the organization. Relationships within the organization affect attitudes, which affect the job. Outside influences may also affect the creation of jobs. Defining roles and properly positioning the job minimizes conflict.

Although the terms *job* and *position* are sometimes used interchangeably, they are not synonymous since each has a distinct definition in personnel work. A position can simply be defined as a collection of tasks and responsibilities which constitute the total work assignment of a single individual in an organization. A job, on the other hand, can be, and usually is, a group of positions that normally involve the same level of responsibilities, knowledge, duties, and skills. Individuals holding that job category may be scattered throughout the library organization. Rarely is there just one person occupying a job category, although it is possible in smaller libraries. Therefore, many employees who are performing similar or slightly different work should be classified under the same job title which includes a group of positions that are sufficiently alike in duties and qualifications to justify grouping them together under a single description. For instance, a library might

5

employ beginning reference librarians both in subject divisions and in a general reference department. They may have slightly different responsibilities and expertise, and certainly would occupy different "positions," but their duties are similar enough to classify them into the same "job" group, Librarian I or whatever the designation might be.

A job, if it is well planned, should consist of tasks that require similar or related skills, knowledge, and ability. As will be enumerated later, those three key elements are constantly referred to in the management literature as SKAs. Each job should be designed to meet the needs of the organization of which it will become a part. The tasks designated for each job should, within that job, be comparable in the education and experience required, as well as level and degree of responsibilities. Tasks assigned to a job should focus upon the accomplishment of a single process and if possible be related to the same subject field or type of materials. Even in smaller institutions where the challenge is greater, since the same processes must be accomplished with fewer people, the number of unrelated tasks assigned to one job should be kept as low as possible. Having said that, there is a counter argument which states that developing a job too narrowly may be detrimental because some tasks can be easily mastered and monotony due to routine can result in lack of motivation. Ideally the scope of a job should be large enough to challenge and encourage the employee to grow in skills and knowledge and to demonstrate abilities qualifying that individual for advancement within the organization. While it is true that many jobs in libraries must be performed according to prescribed policies and procedures, to reflect uniformity or standardization, each employee still should have some latitude to be creative and vary routines, as long as standards are maintained. Each organization must examine these dynamics in that light and apply the principle of job enrichment where appropriate.

Several concepts that include the word "job" require brief definition here, to avoid later confusion:

Job Analysis is that process of observing and recording information about the work performed by a specific employee in a specific position. It is not an attempt to judge how well each individual employee is performing. Analysis is accomplished through systematic observation of the job activities of each person, which is then augmented by interviews with the employee and supervisor. Those activities should then result in a "job description," which is likely to be a generic description developed from observing activities of individuals in several positions with similar levels of requirements.

Job Classification is the process of categorizing positions (after all jobs have been analyzed and descriptions written) according to the type of work performed, the skills required, and the other job-related factors. Classification is accomplished by reviewing jobs, and grouping individuals into a classification hierarchy for the entire staff of the organization.

Job Description is a cumulative step in collecting, verifying, and correlating information about tasks and content of a job. It is a written description which includes the content description of a group of positions. It may be quite detailed or rather brief.

Job Enrichment is important in organizations, such as libraries, where the education level of employees is generally high. A job must allow some latitude for growth and innovation. It should be broad enough to be challenging and satisfying to the individual occupying the position, while meeting the specific requirements of the organization. Staff development is a concept which has evolved from the need for job enrichment.

Job Evaluation is used as a comparison of jobs for classification and pay purposes. Jobs may be measured against a scale of difficulty or relative to other jobs. Several methods may be used, some are described in detail later.

Job Specification sets forth the requirements and personal qualifications specified for those who might be candidates for the job in question. Such things as work experience, skills, and standard responses on tests might be included here, although test scores are less applicable today than in the past.

ANALYSIS

In order to describe a job, certain things must be known about it. Job analysis examines each job in relation to others in the organization. *What*, *how*, and *why* are the questions that must be answered in the analysis process. Evaluation includes such factors as the responsibilities inherent in the position; requirements for successfully performing the duties; and the relationship of a particular job to others in the organization. Job responsibilities must be clearly described and requirements properly analyzed. Only then can the correct job title be applied, as well as a full description of the job, and an equitable monetary grading relative to other positions. The job's parameters must be identified, both at the beginning or input phase and at the output phase or the end of the chain of activities and events that the incumbent is expected to perform. One must know where the work comes from, what the person in the job does with it, and where it goes next. A good way to begin this evaluation process is to list all of the elements or tasks of the job in question. Those should then be grouped together into like categories, some may be performed daily, while others occur only periodically. When that type of information is accumulated and analyzed, the process of describing or redescribing can begin.

There are several approaches to job analysis, from a very basic listing by rank to a much more complex comparison using job factors and point count factors. Since most people using this manual do not have access to specialists or experts to perform the complicated factor analysis, the more basic approaches will be described. A typical approach is to look at the job in relation to several categories—all spelled out later in this text under job description. The most effective way of gathering this data is by asking the incumbents through written questionnaire, or oral/taped interviews, or by observing the activities performed in the work situation. This collected data then forms the basis for reviewing the job.

The interview phase may range from being very structured to a more ad hoc approach. A preset series of questions should be developed to add structure and to elicit most of the relevant information. An open-ended final portion of the interview can elicit data about activities which might be unique to a given position, but also applicable to a job category. Both the set of questions and the approach to interviewing will need to be adjusted to the situation and the individual. The primary goal of the interview is to establish a task inventory. A list, which should have been previously developed by the interviewee, is helpful to focus attention on the grouping of tasks. Also the interviewee should be prepared for the interview by being told the purpose and the outcome. Occasionally it might be beneficial to conduct a group interview with all of the individuals whose positions are likely to fall within the job category. If the person conducting the interview is not the immediate supervisor, an interview should also be scheduled with that supervisor. All of this, of course, requires good interviewing skills. Those are discussed in the next chapter on recruiting.

This process produces a body of factual materials upon which a description now can be based. This brief discussion is simply intended to give an overview of the process, rather than to discuss in detail the many systems for analyzing jobs. It provides enough information for organizations to develop a process which will facilitate describing all jobs in the library. A decision flow chart for developing job analysis might look something like Figure 1.

DESCRIPTION

Once the need for a job has been established and basic background information is gathered, a written description is in order to specify parameters and components of that job. The job description is a cumulative step in collecting, verifying, and correlating information about tasks and content of a job. The basic steps in developing job descriptions are: identifying what the library organization wants to know; gathering the facts as already discussed; organizing the materials according to categories; and writing the description. In preparation for writing the description, one needs to know: what the job is; what mental and physical abilities are required; what preparations are necessary to do the job; what the principal job duties are; how accurate or exacting the work must be; what the consequences of error are; how frequently aspects of the job are performed; what the degree of responsibility is; where the work comes from and where it goes; and what personal contacts are involved, including who supervises and who is supervised by the occupant. The idea of a job description is to compress the largest possible amount of clear, important information in the fewest possible words.

Job descriptions are important not only because they clarify the responsibilities of each position but because they also help employees identify relationships between a particular position and others within the organization so that greater coordination and a unified sense of purpose can prevail. A job description is also the primary basis for determining performance measures. A good, accurate job description is the single most important foundation of personnel activities. It serves several useful purposes:

- Self-development and role identification. Employees can benefit from gathering data and drafting their own descriptions, thereby gaining an appreciation of the job and an understanding of how it relates to others in the total organization.

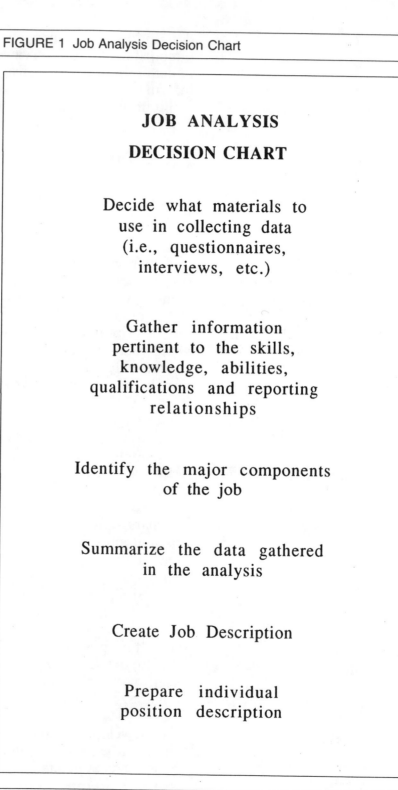

FIGURE 1 Job Analysis Decision Chart

JOB ANALYSIS DECISION CHART

Decide what materials to use in collecting data (i.e., questionnaires, interviews, etc.)

Gather information pertinent to the skills, knowledge, abilities, qualifications and reporting relationships

Identify the major components of the job

Summarize the data gathered in the analysis

Create Job Description

Prepare individual position description

- Team building efforts. It helps others within the organization understand their coworkers various roles, thereby reducing criticism and producing a more supportive atmosphere.
- Work simplification. It enables the organization to identify gaps or overlaps in performance of certain tasks.
- Counseling current employees. It can help staff members experiencing difficulties in meeting requirements stated, as well as exceptionally productive staff members who are developing greater expertise and may be ready for advancement.

The description also provides some information upon which to base an equitable salary scale and to reward merit. Taken as a whole, then, job descriptions can provide a picture of the structure of the library.

Written descriptions can also aid in the placement or removal of employees through the promotion and/or transfer process for those who have performed successfully, as well as the transfer and/or termination process for those who have not. In handling complaints and grievances, as well as conduct of work and discipline, the description can provide guidance. Further, it can be helpful in recruiting efforts and an orientation tool for new employees since a written description should provide the necessary details of the job. The formal performance appraisal process can be linked to the job descriptions which provide a guide to the stated responsibilities, and this will be discussed in greater detail under evaluation. Finally, in regard to health and safety issues the description serves as an important guide.

Job descriptions often set the tone of the organization, since they relate individual responsibilities to the overall objectives of the organization. When developed and applied to an employee, a job description becomes an agreement between employer and employee which, although somewhat flexible and eligible for change as the need arises, should not be so broad and vague as to be useless. In its simplest form it illustrates relationships and related responsibilities within the organization. When looked at in that regard, it can also aid in tracking the work-flow process. When descriptions are not available, work relationships are sometimes questionable, requirements are considered arbitrary and responsibilities are ambiguous and open to interpretation. All descriptions, regardless of what additional thoughts or stipulations an organization might decide to include, contain five general areas:

1. Tasks, or duties and behaviors that are important to the job;

2. Conditions which make relationships and the performance of responsibilities easy or difficult;
3. Standards or performance measures which are expected for each duty;
4. Skills, knowledge, and abilities (the acronym SKA is often used for this unit) required to successfully perform in the job; and
5. Qualifications: education and experience necessary to ensure successful performance of responsibilities.[1]

The relationship of the first three components is demonstrated in Figure 2.

There are several types of job descriptions varying greatly in both detail and focus. Therefore, choosing one or developing a slightly different one for an individual library is a matter of preference depending upon how it will be utilized.

WORK-FLOW ORIENTED JOB DESCRIPTION

This is usually a narrative description which tends to become quite detailed. Since it is not frequently used, it will not be discussed here. A more popular type of description is:

MULTIPURPOSE JOB DESCRIPTION

This description attempts to cover a series of objectives in one statement. It can be developed to include information needed for administrative purposes, for record keeping, and for legal compliance, as well as guidance for individuals. Such descriptions are usually broad and often vague. They most often include:

FIGURE 2 Tasks-Conditions-Standards Comparison

Tasks	Conditions	Standards
Type Correspondence	When asked by supervisors; using an IBM compatible system with wordstar software.	All letters revised to error-free, completed by end of work day, with reasonable lead time.
Greet Visitors	In a friendly manner, refer appointments to designated manager.	No complaints from visitors referred to or waiting before being referred.

Job Title: a generic title usually for a group of positions identical or at least similar with respect to their significant duties. The title should reflect responsibilities and the demands of the job that set it apart from others in the organization. Remember, too, that a job title is distinct from a position.

Position Title: reflects the duties to be performed by a person occupying a single position. This level of specificity is observed in organizations which rely heavily on a centralized office for personnel functions. Generic job descriptions cover all the jobs in a given class whereas an individual position description is written for each incumbent in each specific job. This is a point where the description can be personalized.

Job Summary: a brief two or three sentence summary statement, including the major purpose. It presents a synopsis of the nature of the job and discusses relationships which can be reflected in an organizational chart.

Job Duties and Responsibilities: provides a justification for the existence of the job, perhaps the most important component of the description. It must include a thorough and complete description of what, why, and how the job is done, not just a vaguely worded list of duties but rather a comprehensive statement of the major duties that compose the job. Incidentally, a job, on the average, should have about five such major functions. Four to seven is the usual range. These major duties should be arranged in some logical sequence in the description, either in order of importance or by frequency of performance. These task areas, when taken together, identify the purpose of the job. Figure 3 shows how tasks of a Senior Reference Librarian might be assessed. Each task area should be introduced by a statement that describes type of behavior and outcomes for success in performance. This enumeration identifies for the employee and supervisor the exact tasks for which a person will be responsible. It also indicates to the supervisor those areas that must be supervised and the components for evaluation. For lower level jobs the term "list of responsibilities" is most appropriate, while for higher level jobs it might be classified and thought of as "assignments." Remember, this is a list of responsibilities not the activities through which the employee achieves those responsibilities. It can be thought of in the same hierarchy of performance evaluation diagrammed in Figure 4.

Job Requirements: or specifications include the level of educa-

FIGURE 3 Task Importance Scale: Senior Reference Librarian*

Task	% of Time Spent	Importance on 1-10 scale
1. Supervise 5 other members of Reference Staff	50%	2
2. Identify information needs of patrons in person at desk	25%	1
3. Negotiate needs of patrons via telephone or FAX	15%	3
4. Schedule desk assignments, use of quick reference service	10%	4

*In order of importance, with #1 indicating the most important.

tion; experience; and skills, knowledge, and abilities (SKAs) demanded. It is a statement about the job and conditions of work that are used to establish job difficulty or worth, categorized as:

> *Knowledge,* or the body of information related to a particular subject area facilitating performance;

> *Skills,* defined as an observable capability to perform certain learned motor acts; and

> *Abilities,* that being the facility to perform a physical or mental activity.

Great care should be taken in stating requirements since any requirements for a job should be proven necessary for the successful performance of that job. Sometimes job specifications reflect what the organization would like to have and not what is necessarily applicable to the performance of the job in question. Caution should be exercised in stating minimum qualifications since these are the ones which are most commonly questioned on legal issues. The qualifications required must fairly reflect the most acceptable minimum qualifications, typically stated in terms of specific educational course work, training, or equivalent experience. Any job specification not essential for successful job performance may violate federal or state regulations and should be avoided. A certain progression of relationships exists between those previously mentioned tasks, standards, skills/qualifications, and evaluation which should be evident as one develops the description because:

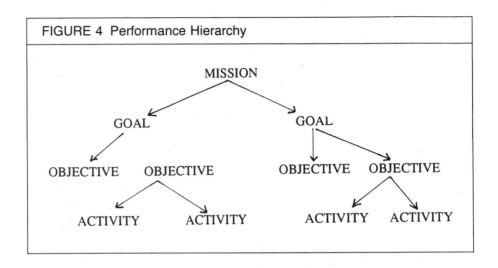

FIGURE 4 Performance Hierarchy

- each task must be performed at a minimal standard for the organization to succeed;
- certain skills, knowledge and abilities enable the employee to perform tasks up to standard;
- certain minimum qualifications ensure that the employee will have those skills, knowledge and abilities; and
- that possession can be tested in the performance evaluation process.

Relationships: included here are the details of the work hierarchy —to whom the incumbent reports, the number of employees or the organizational units supervised by this job, and the internal and external relationships of the job.

Accountabilities: an employee is accountable for every responsibility listed. Authority should define the limits of delegation to the employee, including decision-making limitations and budgetary limitations. This section describes the end results of the job, and may include how success or failure is measured on the job. This reference to standards of performance is sometimes treated separately. It is a statement of how well the employee is expected to achieve each of the primary responsibilities in the job description. If standards are implemented, there should be a cause and effect approach to the writing of this section, i.e., responsibility produces result. Standards define such things as how well, how often, how soon and how accurately, and define the allowable margins of error. This section may also include a probationary period clause which reflects the length of on-the-job training required before the individual is a permanent employee.

Job location: reflects a legal requirement to support selection procedures. Factors in working conditions, such as cleanliness, noise, stress, travel, hazards or safety risks, and other physical requirements are included here.

Date: when the job was last analyzed.

RESULTS-ORIENTED JOB DESCRIPTION

Another way of thinking about descriptions focuses upon performance standards and what is expected to be achieved in the job. It emphasizes three elements:

- an action verb;
- what the action produces; and
- how the tasks are achieved.

Proponents of this approach maintain that duties are better understood if they are expressed in this cause-result kind of relationship. A couple of simple examples are illustrated in Figure 5. A way to express that same relationship is through narrative form: "Provides information users needs by conducting interviews to determine needs and then ascertaining availability of data," and "Hires qualified employees by recruiting and screening applicants." A different way of illustrating this relationship is to compare a Duties-oriented statement to a Results-oriented one, as shown in Figure 6.

Finally one must consider an item frequently found in job descriptions, and that is the "other duties as assigned" clause. Its inclusion is quite controversial, being open to the extremes of

---

FIGURE 5 Example of Cause-Result Description

Duty	Result
Conduct reference interview	Provides appropriate and timely information to patron's request
Recruits and screens applicants for professional positions	Hires qualified professionals

interpretation as either an intent to protect the employer against the "It is not in my job description" syndrome or the employees attempt to slough off work. Some associations and other membership organizations have been known to instruct members to refuse to do work not specified. Both of these potentially polarizing approaches increase rigidity in an organization when flexibility might be more desirable both for the individual and the organization.

A valid argument for excluding this statement relates to evaluation of performance. One might legitimately ask how it is possible to measure performance if the employee is responsible for doing work not specifically designated in the job description. This is an issue which continues to be debated and its application, or lack thereof, continues to be abused by both employer and employee. Each individual organization must decide whether or not to include the statement in its job descriptions, and to determine if it is a legitimate and productive requirement for that organization.

When it comes to actually writing the job description for the first time, or rewriting it to conform to changing circumstances some maintain that it is best to let the employee do the initial writing. If the initial draft is composed by the employee, the argument goes, that person writing the description will identify with the description and thus be more supportive and motivated. For balance, a review of the draft by the immediate supervisor can further add objectivity to the process. However, there are those who maintain that job descriptions must be written by trained job analysts, with employee and supervisor having input through questionnaires or structured interviews. There are good arguments for both approaches, not the least of which is economic. No matter which approach is taken, the process requires commitment and thoughtful analysis. An understanding of what is required, with samples to guide, is sufficient for a start to write job descriptions.

If the initial draft of a description is being written by the individual(s) occupying the job(s), several pointers might be helpful:

- It is important to keep a list of all the different tasks you have performed within a reasonable period of time, say the past two months, assuming that is a time frame that adequately covers most of the responsibilities, realizing that some others are less frequent and would have to be addressed as they are identified.
- Remember that what is being described is what is done on the job, not the individual and his or her personality.

FIGURE 6 Duty vs. Results-Oriented Description[2]

Duties-Oriented	Results-Oriented
Job title: Assistant to the Director	Job title: Assistant to the Director
Reports to: Director	Reports to: Director
Job purpose: Performs administrative as well as some secretarial duties for the library director	Job purpose: Facilitates the work of the director's office by performing administrative duties
Work performed: Perform administrative details of functions assigned to supervisor, thereby supporting the functions within limits of delegated authority	Job results: Provides administrative support for the director by managing staff and procedures as authorized
Initiates and answers correspondence and inquiries on his\her behalf	Acts for the director by initiating and answering correspondence within limits of authority
Makes arrangements, prepares agenda and may act as recording secretary	Facilitates smoothly functioning office by making arrangements and maintaining records
Collects, assembles, and analyzes data for reports, presentations and records	Prepares reports by collecting, assembling and analyzing data
Responsible for the administrative function of the office, such as personnel records and accounts[2]	Accomplishes work of the office by directing secretaries and clerks

- An attempt should be made at creating a hierarchy of duties, with the most important ones listed first.

A few simple suggestions might be helpful:

- Keep the style as simple and brief as possible.
- Omit unnecessary adjectives, articles and other words and avoid phrases that downgrade or degrade.
- Use quantitative words where possible.
- Omit the subject and begin each sentence with an action verb.

The selection of the verb is especially important since it will often denote the level of difficulty of the tasks outlined.

Performance standards, qualifications for the position, authority and accountability are examples of areas of the description that might change over time and need to be reviewed and revised. Therefore, they are never static and should be reviewed periodically.

Job descriptions should be clear and specific in the style of writing and in content. An ideal job description should be no longer than a couple of pages and should include only key elements. Remember, a job description is not a procedures manual, nor can it reflect a detailed statement of how each task is accomplished. A description does not reflect the day-to-day activities that are performed on the job.

To aid in listing these tasks, and in line with the necessity to use action verbs, some popular action oriented verbs are listed in Figure 7.

EVALUATION

Once jobs have been designed and accurately described, each job can be placed within the hierarchical order within the organization. This is usually the point where outside experts, familiar with the various systems of classification, are needed. An attempt should be made to classify each job category according to important skills and abilities required, which then acts as an index of job values within the library. Since this is created partially for pay purposes and pay levels it is based upon a number of factors. Skills, education, experience required, and the amount of end responsibility, are common criteria used in making this evaluation. Each

FIGURE 7 Action Verbs for Job Descriptions

account	code	distribute	issue
acquire	collaborate	draft	itemize
act	collect	edit	justify
activate	compare	employ	keep
add	compile	ensure	lay out
administer	compose	enter	list
adopt	conduct	establish	locate
advise	confer	estimate	maintain
affirm	consider	examine	manage
allocate	consolidate	execute	measure
amend	consult	expedite	meet
anticipate	contact	extend	merge
appraise	contract	figure	negotiate
apprise	contribute	file	note
approve	control	fill	notify
arrange	cooperate	find	observe
assign	coordinate	follow up	obtain
assist	copy	forecast	operate
assume	correct	formulate	order
attach	correspond	furnish	organize
attend	counsel	gather	originate
audit	create	give	outline
authorize	date stamp	guide	oversee
balance	decide	handle	participate
bill	define	hold	pay
budget	delegate	identify	perform
calculate	delete	implement	place
call	describe	improve	plan
cancel	design	index	post
catalog	determine	inform	prepare
charge	dictate	inspect	present
chart	direct	instruct	process
check	disburse	interview	produce
circulate	discharge	inventory	program
classify	discuss	investigate	proofread
close	disseminate	inventory	promote

Continued

FIGURE 7 *Continued*

propose	remove	secure	survey
protect	render	select	tabulate
provide	replace	sell	terminate
publicize	report	serve	test
purchase	represent	service	total
rate	request	sign	tract
receive	require	specify	train
recommend	review	store	transcribe
reconcile	revise	structure	transfer
recruit	route	study	upgrade
refer	sample	submit	verify
register	scan	suggest	visit
reject	schedule	summarize	write
release	screen	supervise	
remit	search	supply	

job may be measured against others in the organization or some attempt can be made to measure them against a designated scale of difficulty designed to qualitatively define skills levels. Jobs also can be ranked relative to the top positions in the organization. Other methods, such as factor method, are more complex because they attempt to relate factors to the degree of job difficulty. Those factors are weighted according to importance, each job is then ranked according to each factor and then quantitative rankings are developed through multiplying weight times rank of each of them. These scores are converted to point values which can then be translated into pay categories. Usually all professional positions fall into one grouping, library associates or paraprofessionals into another, library technicians and clerks into others, and other employees, such as bookmobile drivers or custodians into still another group. Within each group there will be hierarchical levels based upon experience, education and responsibility associated with the job. Other factors to be considered would probably include physical effort and working conditions. A job title is assigned to each level. Jobs requiring the same level of education, experience, and responsibility are given the same title, although the tasks associated with each may be different. For instance, an experienced reference librarian and an experienced cataloger could both be classified as Librarian III. The same procedure is used for all the other job groupings. There is no standard as to how many levels are used in each grouping. In larger institutions there may be many, in smaller ones only a few.

The job evaluation and classification determines relationships among wage and salary rates. The assignment of jobs into categories can be accomplished through various methods:

Point Factor Method is probably the most commonly used method. In this classification scheme, a quantitative point scale is developed which identifies factors involved in a job and assigns weights to the factors. For instance, one factor that is considered is length of experience. A position requiring up to three months might receive 25 points, while one requiring five years might receive 125 points. When the points are totaled, that figure can serve as the basis for assigning a position and salary rate within the hierarchy. Those with the highest number of points are placed at the highest position in a hierarchy, those with the lowest are placed at the bottom of the hierarchy.

Factor Comparison Method is achieved by comparing jobs with each other and also by subdividing jobs into factors that have dollar values attached. Instead of using the point method mentioned above, it uses a monetary scale. In this system key or benchmark jobs are identified and measured against a series of factors. This then presents a framework against which all other jobs can be compared.

Simple Ranking System is a nonquantitative approach that is widely used. It requires a simple ranking of positions based upon comparing one with another. This subjective comparison is intended to establish the overall worth of each position. The reliability of this approach can be enhanced by having the input of several evaluators. This is probably most appropriate in smaller systems. This process, too, creates a hierarchy upon which salary categories can be applied.

Job Classification System is another nonquantitative system in which classes of jobs are defined on the basis of duties, skills, abilities, responsibilities, and other job-related qualities. The jobs are grouped into classes and arranged in a hierarchy from lowest to highest. Extreme caution must be taken to avoid inequities in this approach, particularly since pay rates are likely to be in existence already.

This is not a comprehensive listing of approaches, nor is it recommended that individuals without experience attempt to develop a classification plan, unless it is the simplified ranking one. Nonquantitative plans are less scientific yet might be effective, particularly for smaller organizations. As can be seen, systems range from simple description and listing of jobs by rank, to the most sophisticated structure computing job factors and using point count analysis. It is assumed that most readers will be most interested in the simpler methods which can be conducted in-house by a well prepared staff, rather than a more sophisticated one which requires the expertise of job analysts. For examples of forms see Appendix I.

REFERENCES

1. James Evered, "How to Write a Good Job Description," *Supervisory Management,* v. 26 (April 1981):14-19.

2. Donald E. Klingner, "When the Traditional Job Description is not Enough," *Personnel Journal,* v. 58 (April 1979):246-47.

2 THE LAW

Supervisors should know the laws that pertain to employee selection, job performance and performance appraisal. Although these laws are too numerous and complex for an adequate explanation in this manual, the U.S. Equal Employment Opportunity Commission has issued guidelines for employers in which both legal and illegal practices are described. Copies of these guidelines may be obtained from any local human resources specialist, or directly from the Equal Employment Opportunity Commission in Washington, D.C.

Many laws and other regulations exist at the state and local level, as well as those under purview of the federal government. Everyone involved in personnel matters should be aware of those various regulations and how they affect the workplace. If in doubt, seek information and advice from local, state, or federal offices responsible for monitoring programs. Only federal regulations that have the broadest of application to all segments of the country are discussed in this section.

THE LEGAL ASPECTS

The following discussion is not intended to be a legal treatise or to be perceived as giving legal advice, but rather an overview of important regulations which relate to hiring and performance evaluation. In industry many court cases have been brought to determine the basis upon which things such as promotion, retention, and salary increases are made. The use of personality traits has been addressed in many federal regulations. There are more than two dozen federal laws and numerous state regulations and laws as well as local ones which prohibit discrimination in employment. Only the major federal regulations will be discussed here.

Good personnel practice requires accurate information both about jobs and how individuals are performing in them. Legal requirements for appraisal, basically, point out that such appraisals should be:

- job related and valid;
- collected under formal standardized conditions;
- carefully reviewed to eliminate bias regarding race, color, sex, religion, sexual orientation, age, national origin, handicap, or veteran's status.

To avoid ratings based on vague and subjective factors, evaluations must be based upon job-related performance criteria which are derived from job analysis, and conducted by raters with background and knowledge about the job.

The employer's most potent legal defense of a performance review system or a recruitment process is in the area of job-relatedness. The primary vehicle for demonstrating the job-relatedness of most court decisions about employees is job analysis which is then reflected in job descriptions and measured through performance review. Documentation and use of such data is increasing in proportion to the amount of litigation and regulation in human resource management. Written performance appraisals are important evidence in court. Appraisals constitute "tests" within the framework of "Uniform Guidelines on Employee Selection Procedures" issued by the Equal Employment Opportunity Commission (EEOC) and U.S. Department of Labor. The EEOC's "Guidelines on Employment Selection Procedures" of 1978 require that appraisal systems be job related. Trait-based performance systems under those guidelines cannot be defended and would have difficulty in court. Behavior-based systems, although difficult to defend, do carry validity if they can be developed in direct relationship to job-related criteria. Others which are quantitative are easier to support. Growing numbers of cases involve Equal Pay Act and the Age Discrimination in Employment Act.

Legal considerations require one to be prepared to defend any system instituted, if challenged. Employees are protected by laws that address most work situations. Fair employment is one area which is uniformly addressed on both state and federal levels. No longer does the employment-at-will doctrine, utilized for so many years, automatically apply. Just-cause carries much more legal weight. Employment-at-will requires defense that only the performance appraisal can supply. In addition employees may not be demoted without documented evidence of job failure, evidenced in systematic performance appraisal. Therefore, the appraisal review process is important as evidence of performance and can be defended in demotion, transfer, promotion, or termination.

EEOC GUIDELINES

The Equal Employment Opportunity Commission (EEOC) Guidelines of 1966 and 1970 (with an Act of 1972 which amends Title

VII, to be discussed later) cover all private employers of 15 or more people, all private and public educational institutions, state and local governments, employment agencies, labor unions, and apprenticeship and training programs. Executive Order 11246 of 1965, amended by Executive Order 11375 of 1967, requires government contractors to have written plans of affirmative action to remedy past discrimination. It is administered by the Department of Labor. The EEOC provides guidelines for all others by stating:

> Extensive efforts to develop (affirmative action) procedures, analyses, data collection systems, report forms and file written policy statements are meaningless unless the end product will be measurable, yearly improvements in hiring, training, and promotion of minorities and females in all parts of your organization.[1]

The EEOC has developed guidelines in hiring and performance reviews. They relate to a number of factors shown in Figure 8.

FEDERAL LAWS

Title VII of the Civil Rights Act of 1964: any personnel practice that adversely affects certain classes of individuals is deemed unlawful unless an organization can demonstrate that those policies and practices are justified by business necessity. This is interpreted as meaning the employer must show overriding evidence that a discriminatory practice is essential to the safe and efficient operation of the organization. Once a plaintiff can show a *prima facie* case of discrimination by demonstrating adverse impact upon any protected group, the burden of proof falls on the organization to justify its employment policy. Discrimination against a person, with respect to compensation or privileges of employment, because of the individual's race or color or national origin; or to limit or classify employees in any way which would deprive individuals of employment opportunities or adversely affect his or her status as an employee because of such race, color or national origin is prohibited. This act is administered by the Equal Employment Opportunity Commission (EEOC). The Tower Amendment permits the use of "professionally developed ability tests for employ-

FIGURE 8 EEOC Guidelines

Subject	Illegal	Legal
Lie Detection	Most states ban or regulate the use of polygraph exams. Right to privacy and equal protection of law requires it.	
Health and General Physical Requirements	Prohibit discrimination on basis of physical handicap. Job requiring certain physical abilities may require physical exam, which is lawful.	Some statutes expressly exclude certain conditions from the definition of handicap, for example, alcholic or a drug abuser when current use prevents individual from performing the duties. Also excludes those with currently contagious diseases or infections if they constitute a risk to others. AIDS has been determined a physical handicap in many states.
Race, Color, Religion, National Origin	All unexplained direct or indirect inquiries may be evidence of bias. State laws may expressly prohibit.	Employers may lawfully collect such information for affirmative action programs, government record keeping, and reporting requirements, or studies to promote EEO recruiting and testing. Employers must be able to prove these legitimate business purposes and keep this information separate from regular employee records.
Pregnancy	Cannot use pregnancy or related condition in and of themselves as a reason for rejection.	May be rejected only if the pregnancy prevents individual from satisfactorily performing the duties of position involved.

Continued

FIGURE 8 *Continued*

Honorable Discharge	Illegal to prefer honorable discharge unless proven that requirement has strong relationship to successful performance of job.	
Age	unlawful to discriminate in employment against persons age 40 and over on basis of age.	Not unlawful, but unwise, to ask applicant to indicate age during pre-employment process.
Height and Weight	If minorities or women more often disqualified and meeting height or weight limits not necessary for safe job performance.	
Sex	Inquiries about sex unlawful if limitations are expressed unless based on a bona fide occupational requirement	May be determined in pre-employment inquiry if the inquiry is made in good faith.
Marital Status, Children, Child	Non-job related and illegal if used to discriminate against women. Illegal to ask only women.	If information is needed for tax, insurance, or Social Security purposes, get it after employment.
Sexual Preference	Most states and local laws give rise to claim of violation of constitutional rights.	Distinction has been made between "conduct" and "orientation." No federal law specifically prohibits discrimination on the basis of sexual preference.
English Language Skill	If not necessary for job and minorities are more often disqualified.	

Continued

FIGURE 8 *Continued*

Education Requirements	If not directly job-related or no business necessity is proven and minorities more often disqualified.	Any requirement must relate to the successful performance of the job in question. Some jobs require specialized knowledge.
Friends or Relatives Working for Employer	Preference for friends or relatives of current workers, if this reduces opportunities for women or minorities.	
Arrest Records	If no subsequent convictions and no proof of business necessity. Mere request for, without consideration of, arrest record is illegal	
Conviction Record	May not reject all applicants with arrest and conviction records.	Only if their number, nature, and recentness are considered in determining applicant's suitability. Inquiries should state that record isn't absolute bar and such factors as age and time of offense, seriousness and nature of violation, and re-habilitation will be taken into account. If convicted may be relevant to job (e.g., accountant with recent embezzlement conviction)
Military Service Discharge	Honorable discharge if minorities more often disqualified. Employers should not reject applicants with less than honorable discharges, and inquiry re military record should be avoided unless business necessity is shown.	If information is used to determine if further back-ground check is necessary. Inquiries should state that less than honorable dis-charge isn't absolute bar to employment and other factors will affect final decision.

Continued

FIGURE 8 *Continued*

Citizen-ship	If has purpose or effect of discriminating on basis of national origin.	Employment of unauthorized aliens prohibited. Employer may choose U.S. citizen over legal alien, but may not prefer citizen over highly qualified alien.
Appear-ance and Grooming		May require reasonable standards when applied uniformly, as long as such standards, in a business setting, do not have a disproportionate impact on women and minorities or discrimination on the basis of religion.
Economic Status	Inquiries re poor credit rating are unlawful, if no business necessity is shown. Other inquiries re financial status - bank-ruptcy, car or home owner-ship, garnishments - may be illegal because of dis-parate impact on minorities.	
Avail-ability for Holiday/ Weekend Work		If employer can show that questions have no exclu-sionary effect on employee or applicant who needs consideration for religious practices.
Data Required for Legitimate Business Purposes		Information on marital status, children, etc, necessary for insurance, reporting requirements, and other business purposes should be obtained after the person is employed.[2]

ment decisions, provided that the instrument is not designed, intended, or used to discriminate because of race, color, religion, sex, or national origin." The EEOC has written guidelines (29 CFR Section 1607) with respect to the creation and analysis of tests.

Age Discrimination in Employment Act of 1967, amended in 1974 and 1978: states that no employer can have mandatory retirement plans for employees age 65 or younger. This was later amended to age 70 and now has no cap. In regard to appraisal, this Act's purpose is to help employers and employees to find ways of meeting performance problems arising from the impact of age.

Rehabilitation Act of 1973, amended in 1974 and 1978: states that the mental and physical needs of handicapped individuals must be taken into consideration and reasonable accommodations must be made for both employees and potential employees or applicants. This applies only if the organization has $2,500 or more in government contracts.

National Labor Relations Act of 1935 and the Fair Labor Standards Act of 1938, amended as the Equal Pay Act of 1963 and the Walsh-Healey Act: basically requires employers to pay on an equal system based upon the work done.

Order on Testing and Other Selection Procedures of the Office of Federal Contract Compliance (OFCC), and the Uniform Guidelines on Employee Selection Procedures of 1978: applies to promotions and addresses regulations for selection of employees and legal considerations procedures.

Privacy Act of 1974: guards against illegal use of records about employees. It insures privacy of those records and makes specific reference to both medical and arrest records which might exist. It also permits past and current employees of the government access to their individual records. Several states have similar laws.

Vietnam Era Veterans Readjustment Act of 1972 reenacted in 1974 and ammended in 1976 and 1978: relates to requirements of affirmative action in relation to hiring and promoting disabled veterans and Vietnam veterans. Regulations apply to organizations with $10,000 or more in government contracts.[3]

The above regulations clearly indicate that subjective performance appraisal invites legal questions. If employees are evaluated, clear measures for performance must be established. For instance, any skills required must be accurately used on the job. Courts have thrown out subjective ratings of qualities such as "leadership, appearance, ethical habits, loyalty to the organization," etc. General criteria for appraisal also have been rejected in court, including ones on appearance. From the legal perspective, personnel decisions based on trait measures and affecting protected groups are deemed "susceptible to partiality and to the personal taste, whim, or fancy of the evaluator."[4]

Any appraisal forms and scoring systems used must be objective and standardized. They should be job related, characterized by formal job analysis, administered by trained supervisors and rated by people who have contact with the employee.[5]

Guidelines have been developed to help designers of appraisal forms meet legal requirements. Among the factors to be considered are:

1. Written instructions to accompany forms;
2. Appraisal ratings should be checked for job relatedness and validity;
3. Appraisal measures should be derived through job analysis that appropriately represents all significant performance dimensions;
4. Absence of "adverse impact" on "protected groups" as a result of decisions based on appraisals must be in place and care should be taken through measurement development, training, and ongoing review, to eliminate bias regarding race, color, sex, religion, sexual orientation, and national origin;
5. User orientation and training programs are logical next steps;
6. Appeal and review provisions must be firmly in place;
7. No exclusive reliance on subjective evaluations of supervisors can be tolerated;
8. Ample opportunity for raters to observe ratees must be evident; and
9. Appraisal raters must have personal knowledge and reasonable contact with the job performance being rated.[6]

REFERENCES

1. Equal Employment Opportunity Commission, *Affirmative Action and Equal Employment for Employers*. v. 1. Washington, D.C.: Equal Employment Opportunity Commission, 1974.

2. See Bradford D. Smart, *The Smart Interviewer: Tools and Techniques for Hiring the Best*. New York: John Wiley & Sons, 1989, pp. 114-116; and Gary P. Scholick, *Interview Guide for Supervisors*. 3rd. ed. Washington, D.C.: College and University Personnel Association, 1988, pp. 2-8.

3. Patricia King, *Performance Planning & Appraisal*. New York: McGraw Hill Book Co., 1989, pp. 146-47.

4. Wade vs. Mississippi Cooperative Extension Service. 528F. 2d 416 (7th Circ. 1978).

5. G. L. Lubben, et. al., "Performance Appraisal: The Legal Implications of Title VII," *Personnel,* v. 57 (May-June 1980):12.

6. C. E. Schneider and R. W. Beatty, "Designing a Legally Defensible Performance Appraisal System," in M. Cohne and R. Golembiewski, eds., *Public Personnel Update*. New York: Marcell Dekker, 1984, p. 37.

3 THE STAFF

The key to effective performance and maximum productivity is the right match of the person to the job. This is a challenging task in today's changing work environment. The nature of the work performed in libraries has been transformed by various applications of technology. The skills and abilities needed today are different from those needed a decade ago. Support staff and librarians now carry out many responsibilities that require some knowledge of computer and other electronic applications. Effective interpersonal skills, particularly the ability to interview users successfully in order to determine exactly what they need, have become critical skills for public services staff. These are only two examples of significant skills that emerged in the past decade for library staff. More changes in the tasks to be performed and in the skills required to perform them can be expected in the decade ahead.

The role of the key professional, the librarian, in libraries and other information centers is evolving. Librarians and information specialists need to work more directly with their clientele. They must anticipate as well as respond to changing needs for information and be more creative in how this is done, especially when financial resources are limited. Librarians have the expertise to help everyone cope with the information explosion. Will that be their role in the future, or will they be replaced by other information specialists? How does a library organization recruit and select the right kinds of individuals to make this all happen?

The changing role of the librarian has direct implications for support staff. Support staff increasingly will be expected to provide more direct support to the librarian. As they assume greater responsibility for such functions as cataloging and providing basic reference service, the clerical work and more routine technical work will disappear.

Changes in work and roles require the job descriptions to be flexible and dynamic. Managers and supervisors must take care to design jobs that will be challenging and meaningful and to describe them so that incumbents will have a clear understanding of what they are expected to do. Good job design and well written job descriptions are the basis for recruitment and selection of the best possible staff.

Library managers must be skilled in job design, but also in "job-matching," that is in matching the tasks and skills required for the job with the person who has those skills. Success in the job-matching process depends upon finding the person who has both the competence to perform the job and the commitment, interest, and motivation to perform effectively.

RECRUITMENT

The goal of every recruitment effort is to attract the best possible pool of qualified candidates for the position. The recruitment process includes advertising the vacancy, soliciting applications and nominations of qualified candidates, and reviewing the applications received.

A recruitment plan should be developed to ensure a pool of qualified candidates. It should at least include:

- Identification of places where advertisements will be placed;
- A timetable for the process;
- A list of special efforts to be made, including the steps to be taken to identify qualified minority candidates; and
- The specific responsibilities of everyone involved in the process.

One of the first decisions to be made is the scope of the recruitment effort. The question should be asked, is this a position for which a national search will be undertaken or is it one for which a regional or local search will be sufficient? The answer will guide both the selection of places to advertise and the overall timetable. Regional or local searches suggest targeted mailings of the vacancy announcements, advertisements in area newspapers and newsletters, and a shorter time frame for the process. The critical decision whether to mount a national search should result from a careful assessment of the probability of attracting a strong pool in a regional or local search.

The *position description* is developed from the *job description* previously discussed, but it is a refinement to relate the parameters of the job description to a particular position in the library. This source document can then be used for writing the advertisement or the vacancy announcement. The description of responsibilities in any advertisement or vacancy announcement should correspond to those listed in the position description. The required qualifications must correspond. Any experience, skill or knowledge that is required must be specified in any advertisement of the vacancy. Careful attention should be given to determining what the actual job requirements are and to making sure that they are specified in all written descriptions of the job.

Advertisements for journals, newspapers, and newsletters, as well as position vacancy announcements, should be written carefully. They should include information about the key responsibilities, all required qualifications, any preferred qualifications, and instructions about how to apply for the position.

The advertisement should be informative and attractive to potential candidates. The language should be clear and precise. A statement about the library's commitment to affirmative action and equal employment opportunity should be included. Information about available benefits is helpful. The minimum salary or salary range should be specified in most cases. Some journals, such as those published by the American Library Association, require that the minimum salary be stated in all advertisements accepted for publication.

The next important step is to select the right places to advertise. It is important to know the range of possible journals, newsletters, and special publications. Selection should be based on a knowledge of which ones are most likely to reach the potential candidates for the position. *American Libraries* is a popular choice because it is sent to every member of the American Library Association. *Library Journal* also reaches a wide national audience. Some library divisions of ALA have publications which include job advertisements. Other specialized publications to consider are *The Chronicle of Higher Education* and *ASIS Jobline*.

Local and regional newspapers, job lines operated by schools of library and information service and library and information associations, and special mailings to library directors, personnel officers, library school deans and placement offices, and other special groups can be very useful sources of applicants. Special efforts to consider include: soliciting nominations, formally by letter, or informally by telephone, from colleagues at other libraries and specialized groups such as the ALA Black Caucus, REFORMA, The Asian-Pacific Library Association (APALA), and others, and the use of placement services and local and national conferences, such as those sponsored by the American Library Association and the Special Libraries Association.

A closing date should be specified to allow enough lead time, especially when the job is advertised in library journals which have lengthy deadlines for publication. If the deadline is flexible, wording should be chosen to reflect that possibility. Language such as "To be assured of consideration, apply by (date)" alerts applicants to a deadline, but also allows the employer discretion to accept "late" applications. An alternative might be: "Applications will be accepted until the position is filled."

Specify a resume should be submitted with a cover letter, or whether an application form is required. Normally, three references are sufficient and any announcement should specify whether names of references are requested. At the time of application, identification of references should be made. Actual letters of reference should be solicited for the specific position and only for serious candidates. Following this practice also helps to reduce the burden of writing letters for those who are called upon to provide them. The process should also identify the person to whom letters of application should be sent and a complete address should be provided.

At this early planning stage it is very useful to clarify the roles and responsibilities of everyone who will be involved in the hiring process. It is likely that among them will be the hiring supervisor, the department head, the library director, the personnel officer if one exists, the members of the search committee, if one is used, and others identified as appropriate for a successful search.

Applications should be reviewed as they are received and categorized, eliminating those individuals who clearly do not meet the minimum required, stated qualifications. A list of selection criteria to guide the process is always helpful. The criteria can be separated into two categories: 1) required qualifications, those that are essential to effective performance needed at the start of employment; and 2) desirable or preferred qualifications, those that are not essential but would be useful. Creation of a grid or chart that lists the selection criteria and the names of applicants is a useful tool.

Each application should be carefully reviewed and assessed. This process will identify the most qualified candidates. In most cases a small number, usually between five and ten applications, will emerge as a pool of the most qualified candidates. If this initial assessment yields a satisfactory group of qualified applicants, the process can move to the next stage. If the pool is not sufficient or rich enough or representative enough, steps should be taken to enrich the pool, by extending the search, soliciting additional nominations, more advertising, or starting over.

References will need to be obtained at this stage for the top candidates. This is normally done by sending a letter requesting a written response or by placing a telephone call. It is very helpful for the person providing the reference to have a copy of the position description.

The letter of request should describe the key responsibilities of the position and should emphasize the critical position requirements. A copy of the full position description should be included along with a statement of a specific date by which the response is required. Some indication should be made as to whether the letter will be kept confidential.

If the reference is to be solicited by telephone, arrangement should be made in advance for a convenient time for the discussion. An outline of the questions should be prepared in advance. Each question must be relevant to the job to elicit an assessment of the applicant's qualifications for the job, not the applicant's personality. At the beginning of the interview it should be established what the relationship is between the reference and the individual candidate in regard to the person's work. Careful attention should be given to the answers to critical information questions. Notes or, if prearranged, recorded tape should be kept when probing for the vital information on the candidate's qualifications. Care should also be taken not to reveal any confidential information about the candidate in this conversation.

When the preliminary reference checks have been completed, it must be decided who will be invited to interview for the position. Usually three or four candidates are selected for the initial round of interviews. Time is an expensive component in the process because care is required in preparing for the interview and in conducting the interview. In some situations it may be prudent to interview only one candidate, if that person is clearly an outstanding candidate and ranks highly above all others.

Supervisors and others involved in the process should be well informed about the policies, procedures, and practices for interviewing in the library organization. The personnel officer, if there is one, or the library director has the responsibility for making certain that they are followed carefully.

THE INTERVIEW

PLANNING

Determine who will meet the candidates. Set the actual schedule for the interview. Every effort should be made to follow the same general schedule for each candidate. Fair and consistent treatment of each is an important principle to follow. Prepare a written schedule that identifies the participants by name and title and also details the time segment and the location of each appointment. Include time for a tour of the library or information center, a visit to the actual work area, and rest breaks between appointments.

Arrange for private interview space free from interruptions. An hour to an hour-and-a-half is usually required for an in-depth interview, and longer periods should be avoided.

Confirmation should be made about the arrangements for the interview, in writing, to the applicant well in advance of the set interview date. Enclose copies of the schedule and the position description. It is useful also to include some background material on the library and the parent institution. Consider this "interview packet" as information that will both help prepare the candidate for the interview and stimulate interest in the position, the library, and the community. When out of town travel is required, specific instructions on how arrangements will be made and what costs will be covered by the library should be detailed for the applicant.

All who will be involved in the interview should be well prepared. A copy of the application, the position description, the list of selection criteria, and the candidate's schedule, should be provided for each member of the interviewing group. If the interviewer is not experienced in interviewing, some preparation may be necessary. Provide training to those who may need it. It is helpful to review both basic policies and procedures as well as the appropriate and inappropriate areas of questioning with everyone involved in the process. They should be aware of EEOC Guidelines and know what they can and cannot legally ask in the interview. Even the more experienced and skillful interviewers will benefit from this process.

Each interviewer should know how and when to report comments they might have. The best practice is to do so immediately following each interview. Each candidate should be assessed against the same selection criteria, rather than against the other candidates. This individual assessment following each interview will provide the most useful information for the hiring supervisor.

CONDUCTING THE INTERVIEW

The main purpose of the interview is to obtain as much information as possible about the candidate's qualifications for the position. The preparation for an interview is critical to assure that the interviewer gets the information needed for the selection decision. The following guidelines serve as a checklist for supervisors in preparing and conducting the interview:

1. Know the job and what is required to perform it effectively. A thorough job analysis with an accurate specification of selection criteria is very important.
2. Develop and use an interview guide to assure that all the right questions are asked.

3. Follow all legal requirements and guidelines. Ask questions that are relevant to the job and ask the same questions of all candidates. Be fair and consistent in the treatment of all candidates. Document reference checks. Take careful notes in the interview.

4. Be aware of any biases or prejudices. Do not let them influence the interview, the analysis or the final decision.

5. Look for patterns in the interview responses, information obtained in the checking of references and past experience. Consider what these patterns may suggest about the candidate's work patterns, skills, and abilities.

6. Be alert to nonverbal behavior cues. Prolonged silence, lack of eye contact, heavy perspiration, and fidgeting can be the results of nervousness. If prolonged, however, they may indicate that the candidate is not being candid or is someone who is generally not at ease with others.

7. Look for indications of potential in a candidate. The interview is often the best opportunity to assess potential. This assessment is particularly useful when evaluating the candidate against the preferred selection criteria.

Interview questions should be designed to elicit this information and to build on what was provided in the candidate's resume and letter of application. The interview provides the best opportunity to assess a candidate's suitability for the position, and to answer the question, "Is the candidate the right match for the position?"

There is no one best list of questions that would serve any employment interview. A list of specific questions should be developed for the particular position. There are questions that are inappropriate or illegal in any situation. As a general rule, one should ask questions that directly relate to the job and ask the same questions of each candidate. Some general guidelines are listed in Figure 9.

Other points should be considered in conducting an effective interview:

1. Set the right tone. The climate should be a supportive one, rather than adversarial. The whole interview depends upon this initial phase. Establish rapport at the start. Spend about five or ten minutes in

FIGURE 9 Principles for Effective Interviewing

Suggestion	Consequence of Failure to Achieve
Establish rapport with the candidate	The candidate is hesitant, awkward, etc.
Concentrate on the candidate's qualifications, not personality	The interviewer finds out irrelevant personal data, but not about qualifications.
Listen more than talking	The interviewer fails to obtain needed information.
Allow time to observe behavior and response	The interview is superficial and does not get needed data.
Carefully interpret information obtained	Wrong impression can be drawn about candidate
Be aware of biases	Failure to do accurate assessment because of attention to physical features, ethnicity, etc.
Avoid creating a stressful situation	A flustered or defensive applicant will be less able to provide the information needed.
Maintain control of the interview, or carefully regain it	The questions aren't answered and information is not provided.
Ask open-ended questions	Candidate is monosyllabic and tends to withdraw.
Avoid leading statements	These may prompt the candidate to say what the interviewer wants to hear, rather than give honest answers.

this opening phase. Begin with an easy question such as, "Why does this particular job interest you?"

2. An explanation should be given as to how the interview will be conducted. Make the candidate aware of the time frame and how much will be spent on each segment.

3. Describe the purpose of the interview, focusing on a mutual exchange of information. Explain, in some detail, the job and its key requirements. The interviewer wants to learn as much as possible about the candidate and why he or she is interested in the job. At the same time one would assume that the candidate wants to learn all about the job, the unit of work and the library or information center in general.

4. Specify whether the candidate is expected to ask questions as the interview proceeds, or rather wait until the end of the interview. At any rate, encourage the candidate to ask questions at whatever the appropriate point is in the interview.

5. Follow the interview guide or outline which has been developed from the position description and the application form. Formulate questions about educational background, work history, working relationships with supervisors, staff and colleagues. Career plans and interests and a self-appraisal of strengths and weaknesses, as well as suitability for the current position, should be explored.

6. Avoid asking too many questions and be careful not to interrupt the answers. Nevertheless, be sure to ask follow-up questions as needed to get the information being sought. Some skilled interviewers ask four or five general questions in an hour. Remember, the key objective is to get the candidate to talk and to provide the information needed to make a decision on hiring.

7. Allow for pauses in response to questions. Ask the question, then give the candidate time to respond and let the gentle pressure be on the person to talk. Silence is often an indication of preparation for a thoughtful response.

8. Take some notes, enough to create a paper trail and refresh memory, but not so many that it will be distracting to the candidate.

9. About five or ten minutes should be allowed in the final phase to bring the discussion to a close. The next steps in the process should be explained, including how the decision will be made and when the candidate might expect to be notified. A tentative time frame allows for changes which might be necessary. Invite the candidate to call if he or she has questions following the interview. Some situations may permit a follow-up call regarding the progress of the decision. This should be instituted only if one is prepared to take the calls. Finally, the candidate should be thanked for coming.

10. Always keep in mind that one of the candidates is a future employee, and this interview is the beginning of an organizational relationship with that person.

Many libraries conduct multiple session interviews, ones in which candidates meet with several individuals or groups. The individuals involved then advise the hiring supervisor. This approach can be very useful. It also affords an opportunity for different staff to meet and assess the candidates, which not only brings a variety of perspectives to the selection process, but also gives candidates a chance to meet more staff and learn more about the library as well as the position.

SELECTION

Upon completion of the interview, all of the information gathered about each of the final candidates must be carefully and thoroughly analyzed. The accumulated documentation must be reviewed, including: the resume or application form, the letter of application, letters of reference, notes of telephone reference checks, and notes taken during or following the interviews. In analyzing this information, it is very important to focus on the job requirements and the selection criteria that have been established for the position. Each candidate's qualifications should be assessed carefully against these standards.

Everyone who was involved in the interview should be consulted and opinions solicited. Ask for a written assessment of each of the candidates whenever possible. This forces a more careful evaluation of each candidate and provides a record of the evaluation process. The total view may point out areas where there is missing information or concern. It may be useful to conduct another round of in-depth telephone reference checks at this stage. It will provide both the opportunity to learn more about the candidate and to ask questions about any area of uncertainty.

The goal of the selection decision is to identify the best possible candidate for the position. A great deal of information has been gathered and analyzed thus far. With all of that data in hand, the question can be asked, "Is there a clear choice?" If the answer is yes, the decision can be made. If the answer is no, reasons must be explored: Is more information needed? Why is there no clear choice? Is there uneasiness or uncertainty? Is it intuition? If so, work to identify specific reasons for any intuitive feelings. Such reflection may result in the decision either to select a candidate or to continue the search process. Given the critical importance of the hiring decisions, supervisors should take whatever time is needed to make the right decision. Be certain of the choice of a candidate before an offer is extended.

The job should be offered to the selected candidate as soon as possible. This offer should be made by telephone and confirmed in writing immediately thereafter. The offer should include the salary, title or rank of the position, and any other specific terms and conditions of employment. The starting date should be discussed and confirmed, if possible. The library should be prepared to allow time for the candidate to consider the offer. It is best to agree on a short period for that consideration. Both parties should agree to keep confidential the offer and its terms. This agreement about confidentiality is particularly important for the employer, who probably will want to offer the position to another candidate, should this candidate decide not to accept.

A letter which confirms the offer should spell out the specific terms of the position and include any other information that the candidate might need, such as information about moving arrangements, benefits programs, or help in finding housing. The letter should require a written acceptance of the offer from the candidate.

Once the acceptance of the offer has been confirmed, other candidates should be notified of the decision. Candidates who were interviewed will appreciate a personal telephone call with this information, others may be notified by letter. Whenever possible, tell the applicants who the successful candidate was.

The appointment then should be announced to library staff and others in the community. Announcements of appointments to professional positions should be sent to publications such as

Library Journal, American Libraries, and any local publications read by the library's constituents. Some libraries have developed a press release form for this purpose.

RETENTION

As soon as a new staff member arrives, the supervisor should work with that person to ensure a smooth transition and to make the employment experience a long and successful one. From the very beginning, the supervisor should make every effort to help the new staff member learn about the job, the unit, the library, and how to become an effective member of the organization. An orientation program for the employee should be designed to orient the person to the organization as a whole. The first few months' experience will be critical in laying the foundation for a happy and rewarding association or, if done incorrectly, possibly planting seeds of discontent. This would likely be reflected in the performance evaluation process.

Performance planning with the new employee should be started by the supervisor during the first week. Responsibilities should be explained and performance expectations should be communicated clearly and, if feasible, in writing. This early orientation to the job is the start of the performance planning cycle with the person. The other stages in this cycle include:

1. Setting clear goals and objectives for each area of responsibility or job activity. Specific standards or performance expectations for each objective should be defined. A written performance plan that lists the specific objectives, priorities, standards, and time frames should be prepared. Include a schedule for follow-up and mention any ways in which the supervisor will provide support.
2. Training the person to perform each job activity and providing whatever information may be needed is vital. Develop a written training plan that specifies what will be learned and when. Identify who will provide the actual training.
3. Monitoring performance and providing regular, constructive feedback is necessary. Identify success as well as areas for improvement. Address problems as

they occur and alter plans where needed. Retraining may be necessary and appropriate.

4. Scheduling periodic conferences about performance is useful. Discuss what is going well and what is not. Analyze reasons for those successes and failures. Provide guidance and direction as needed. Discuss past performance and agree on a plan for the future. The Periodic Planning Conference (PPC) is one model for these discussions.

PERIODIC PLANNING CONFERENCE

The Periodic Planning Conference (PPC) was developed by Dr. Thomas Gordon and has proven to be an effective approach to performance appraisal and improvement. It is a regularly scheduled conference held by a supervisor with a staff member, usually every three to six months, for thirty minutes to two hours.

The primary purpose of the conference is to develop a plan for the staff member's job activities in order to improve performance, develop new skills and abilities, learn more about the job, and make any changes necessary to carry out the responsibilities of the position. It is also an opportunity for the staff member to suggest ways in which the supervisor can help the individual achieve the performance objectives for this next period and for discussion of any concerns or problems. It is conducted at intervals between the more formal performance evaluations. The program has several characteristics set forth in Figure 10.

There are several assumptions underlying the PPC:

• The individuals and the organization must both change to progress;
• Learning is fun and most people like to learn new things; and
• There is usually a better way of doing things.

Experience with the PPC has proven that each time staff members review the functions and goals of their positions, they do a better job of stating them, measuring them, and achieving them. Thoughts to keep in mind are that:

• No one is ever working at one hundred percent capacity—perhaps no one can—but the evidence is that most people, even those who are effective, are only working at a fraction of their true capacity.
• Change, growth, and modification are inevitable characteristics of an effective organization.

FIGURE 10 Characteristics of the PPC

* a focus on future performance
* a focus on the position responsibilities, performance objectives, and work projects
* open communication and an exchange of information between the supervisor and the staff member
* active participation by the staff member in planning work activities
* a joint approach to problem-solving
* attention to the development and growth of the individual staff member
* a view that mistakes are learning opportunities
* conflict and disagreement are addressed

- People are not strongly motivated to accomplish objectives set by others.
- People work hard to accomplish objectives they set for themselves. There may be some exceptions—some staff will be frightened of the prospect of setting their own objectives, others may be suspicious of the supervisor's motives.
- People are happier when given a chance to accomplish more. A sense of accomplishment—the feeling that they have done something worthwhile—brings most people pleasure and a sense of importance. The more often they can experience these satisfying feelings, the more interested and enthusiastic they will become and the more they will attempt to repeat the experience. The challenge to the supervisor is to see how frequently staff can be given such opportunities.

In both the periodic conference mentioned above and the formal performance evaluation process, a determination should be made of any training or development needs. All of this takes time and both the time and the budget must be provided for this training and development. The conduct of the formal performance evaluation, discussed in the next chapter, completes the cycle. Use this as the opportunity for developing the performance plan for the next period of time. A guiding principle for the supervisor and employee should be that there are no surprises at the end of the evaluation period for the employee about his or her performance. All performance problems should have been discussed and solutions agreed upon well in advance.

The most important factors contributing to retention of staff are meaningful work and an effective relationship with the supervisor. The essential elements for a successful relationship between staff and the supervisor are:

- Partnership, through the empowerment of staff
- Commitment to producing a result, by enacting a vision
- Belief in individual responsibility and mutual respect
- Compassion, generosity and nonjudgmental acceptance
- Listening and speaking for action
- Honoring the uniqueness of each staff member
- Sensitivity to team as well as individual needs
- Belief in lifelong learning and that mistakes are opportunities for learning.

DEVELOPMENT

The need to retain staff and the changing nature of work in libraries have made staff development more important. A formal program designed to support the achievement of organizational goals through the development of staff skills and abilities should be an integral part of the library's human resources program. An established, formal program will help staff, supervisors and the library keep pace with the demand for new skills and knowledge.

Comprehensive planning for staff development in the library provides benefits for the organization and the individual. Among the benefits to the library are:

- A systematic way to identify development and training needs across the library.
- Facilitates the process of updating staff skills and abilities as programs and services change.
- Supports the achievement of library goals, especially in the pursuit of better service to users.
- Promotes more effective use of staff resources.
- Reduces turnover among staff.

Such a program also helps supervisors by providing a framework for planning to address staff training and development needs; encouraging a system-wide approach to work and job design; and identifying available programs and specifying the resources available.

Individual staff members benefit through participating in the programs and by being part of an organization that recognizes the importance of development for staff. A formal program helps staff be better prepared for changes in their work and in the library. Learning is recognized as an ongoing part of the job. The staff have a better understanding of the opportunities available for growth, development, and advancement. The intent of this handbook is not specifically to discuss staff development, but it is such an important part of the whole review process, that it must be briefly mentioned here.

The guiding principles for an effective library staff development program would include:

1. Establish a well-defined set of organizational goals, objectives and priorities for staff development that are an integral part of the library's overall plan.
2. Carefully assess the staff's capacity to meet the organizational objectives.
3. Determine the staff's participation in the staff development needs identification process and the setting of priorities for the program based upon both organizational needs and the staff's perceptions of their own needs.
4. Define the roles and responsibilities of the various staff groups and individuals involved.
5. Assure the library's organizational commitment to staff development by issuing a policy statement.
6. Provide the necessary allocation of resources—personnel, budgetary, and time and energy.
7. Devise a system or process to evaluate program effectiveness.
8. Document the various program components in a staff development program description and distribute this to the staff on a regular basis.

In order to follow those principles, guidelines must be formulated for starting the staff development program. A brief statement of the library's policy on staff development and the goals of the program must be developed. In order to do this, the responsibilities and roles for staff development must be recognized. At the same time the needs in the library must be analyzed by:

FIGURE 11 Staff Development Activities

ACTIVITY	DESCRIPTION
Job definition, job design, and staff selection	This would include defining job competencies; designing jobs that have variety and offer staff meaningful and challenging work; and developing a training agenda.
Orientation to the work unit and library	This would include scheduling informational meetings; developing seminars; producing slide/tape programs or computer assisted programs; organizing tours; creating handbooks, manual and other needed documents; and informal meetings with colleagues.
On the job training	This would include developing a manual of job procedures; promoting individual skills training and coaching by supervisors; encouraging instruction and assistance from co-workers and other colleagues; and formal class sessions.
Personal and professional development	This includes attendance at conferences; eligibility for research leaves or sabbaticals; participation in workshops and institutes; and preparation of seminars and forums on new activities, trends and developments.
Performance planning and assessment	This would include setting goals, objectives and priorities; preparing performance plans; and preparing a personal development plan.

- Considering the organizational framework for staff development: the management philosophy of the library; the attitudes, values and preferences of staff; and the needs of the library vs. those of the individual.
- Determine the training and development needs in relation to current functions and activities as well as in light of anticipated developments: assess the technical, human relations, administrative, conceptual, and problem-solving skills required; examine the needs at organizational, departmental or unit, and individual levels.
- Inventory and describe current programs and opportunities: note the scope, content, and results of each program or activity already available; compare the results to the goals and objectives

of an overall program. The available resources might include in-house library and parent organization programs, as well as those at the local, regional, and national level. Consultants might have also contributed to the process, or if not their services should be considered.

- Determine what is needed to meet the new and emerging needs. A written program statement can then be developed which includes: philosophy, policy and an outline of the activities— i.e., objectives, target group, timetable, and responsibilities.

All of these points are discussed in greater deatil in the following chapter. For examples of selection and staff development forms see Appendix II.

4 THE PERFORMANCE

A performance appraisal system that emphasizes planning through the establishment of performance goals and objectives is much more effective than one that focuses on just appraisal. To perform effectively staff members need to know what is expected and how well they are expected to perform. A careful plan, developed jointly by the supervisor and the staff member, is critical to effective performance and an accurate appraisal of that performance.

Staff involvement in the formulation of goals and objectives is important for individual motivation and commitment. As supervisors in libraries become more removed and less knowledgeable about the details of the work performed by staff, the staff have more direct and accurate information about work requirements. Commitment develops through active participation in setting goals and objectives. A few definitions might be helpful before a full discussion of performance planning and assessment:

Performance goals: are written statements of what an individual expects to achieve in a given period of time. Goals relate to specific position responsibilities and to special projects or new programs or activities. They are general statements that tell what conditions are desirable in the performance of an individual or what he or she is expected to achieve.

Performance objectives: are specific, written statements of what an individual will do to achieve a performance goal. Effective performance objectives are clearly stated; realistic; challenging, yet achievable; and readily understood and accepted by the staff member and the supervisor.

Performance standards or indicators: define the expected level of achievement for each performance objective. Standards describe the quality (how well), the quantity (how much), the rate or percentage, or the time frame expected.

A performance plan: brings together the written statements of goals, objectives, and standards of performance and describes what is expected in the performance of the individual for the coming period of time, usually six months to a year.

THE PLAN

In these days of accountability, performance appraisal is one major necessary component in measuring organizational effectiveness. It is a way of merging what individuals do and how they perform with the overall goal of efficient, effective library service. In for-profit institutions this has been a reality, while in not-for-profit libraries it is becoming more important and necessary. Performance appraisal is a process used to measure and otherwise evaluate an individual employee's accomplishments and behavior over a set period of time. The purpose of such an appraisal is to improve performance and to reward good performance through promotion, favorable transfers and/or merit increase, and, conversely, to point out areas needing improvement for those employees who do not meet expectations. Performance appraisal can, in a way, be viewed as a test, because most procedures and practices relating to personnel decisions are tests in the strict meaning of the law.

This review process is typically a joint effort of the employee and the immediate supervisor who is most familiar with work accomplished and future directions which will benefit both the employee and the institution. It is not simply a process of filling out another form, which takes place on a Tuesday afternoon when nothing else important is happening. Rather, it should be viewed as a complex but satisfying process of self-knowledge and motivation. A systematic, written performance appraisal system provides a sound method of distinguishing among the performances of employees. If a personnel office exists in the organization, impetus and coordination should come from that office and a personnel officer should be responsible for making sure that each person in the organization understands the significance of and benefits from a performance appraisal process. In this regard, basic training sessions for all who will be involved in evaluating others are useful. A training program would provide information such as the rationale behind the system, the policies and procedures to be followed in conducting evaluations, an explanation of the terms to be used on the evaluation form and any other materials necessary for a successful process.

Performance appraisal can be both developmental and/or judgmental in nature. Both aspects are controls to monitor performance and goal attainment and serve as communication devices to foster individual growth and development. Evaluation can be used by both the administration and the employee to monitor progress of individuals on the one hand and as guides in rational decision-making about personnel on the other. As administrative tools they provide guidance for promotion and merit increases, as well as transfer, demotion, or termination. The process is intended to tell the individual how he or she is doing and what needs improvement in the performance of responsibilities. If termination is to be based upon poor performance, formal appraisal is the most objective, documented defense an organization has at its disposal.

Appraisal should be a regular part of the training process to encourage the growth and development of individuals. For training and appraisal to be successful, employees must want to learn to improve their performance, and supervisors must be able to teach and to help employees raise the level of their performance. As employees respond to continued training, they can progressively increase their value to the organization and thus prepare themselves for promotion. Identification of weaknesses can help employees to develop their ability to learn and adapt themselves to new work methods and changing environments.

Performance appraisal, used correctly, is one of the supervisor's most powerful tools. Without the transfer of information embodied in a review process, and the development of a remedial process or plan, the employee cannot be expected to achieve improvement or redirection in performance. The basic question is why it is necessary to conduct performance appraisals. The answer to that question varies from organization to organization, but the most likely response is in order to to increase employee productivity and enhance a sense of accomplishment and contribution to the organization, as well as an effective feedback mechanism in the employee-employer interaction. If it is fully and effectively employed, it can become a contract between the supervisor and employee for future work.

Much advice has been given on the how and why of performance analysis. Guidelines and comments usually fall into several categories:

1. Conduct a job analysis to ascertain characteristics necessary for successful job performance.
2. Incorporate these characteristics into a rating instrument.
3. Train supervisors to use the rating instrument properly.
4. Review of ratings by upper-level or human resources management personnel is desirable.

5. Establish a formal appeals mechanism for those with grievances.
6. Provide some form of performance counseling or corrective guidance to assist poor performers in improving their performance.[1]

As accountability has become more important, evaluation to meet new challenges has become imperative. Performance evaluation processes are good basic output measures for libraries. Although they force the development of policies and procedures which may not yet be in place, it is obvious that those are necessary procedures to move organizations toward developing their most important human resources. Evaluation can be used in many ways, from counseling and employee development to documentation for the organization's effort to meet federal, state, and local employment guidelines.

Evaluation, unfortunately, is sometimes resisted by both managers and employees alike. A most frequently cited reason is that the evaluator lacks the necessary skills, particularly in listening. The argument continues that there is no time now to coordinate an effective evaluation process, since the primary focus must be on getting the work done. Further, it is recognized that some managers have little interest in developing staffs, while others don't like to criticize people who work for them, and still others seem to believe that human nature fosters the harboring of grudges when the truth is written. Finally, some believe that these workers become defensive and suspicious of every action and that any criticism may result in lower, rather than improved, performance.

These attitudes are sometimes reflected in how the evaluation is conducted and ultimately used; in fact some just go through the motions of evaluation with no intention of using it to improve performance while others simply forget about filling out forms, which is another way of resisting the process. Equally discouraging are those who turn the whole review over to the one to be rated without comment or explanation, and accept what is written.

Of all the reasons given for evaluation, the obvious ones include:

1. For promotion purposes, to be able to make a placement or promotion decision based upon identifying strengths and areas needing improvement. The evaluation can facilitate the promotion of outstanding workers, and help weed out or transfer low performers.
2. Equally important is the notion that the process may be tied to consideration of a merit increase, despite the

knowledge that the appraisal is not a salary review. However, many organizations relate at least some decisions about size and frequency of pay increases to an employee's performance appraisal rating.

3. As a basis for disciplinary action, where documentation has been meticuously accumulated and can be defended.

4. Less frequent, is the need for a recorded statement of performance in order to establish a paper trail for internal purposes.

5. The process can aid in a plan for staff development by identifying deficiencies of individual performances.

6. It can provide feedback to employees, enabling an individual to improve performance in the future because he or she is aware of weaknesses and how to correct them.

7. It can improve communication through encouragement, motivation and developmental counseling and from the organization's perspective, help determine both organizational change and individual training needs; and finally

8. To validate the selection process used by the library, or in other words to determine whether the selection process for new employees is working.

The appraisal of one person by another is never totally "scientific," rather tending toward nonexactness and subjectiveness. For this reason the evaluation process always involves some ethical questions. Informal appraisals of employee performance takes place whenever a supervisor says, "I think X is a better employee than Y, and therefore deserves a merit increase." The major, legitimate objection to this kind of appraisal is that without systematic information, regularly gathered and periodically reviewed by the employee and employer, it is almost impossible for a supervisor to be fair and objective. Moreover, it is difficult for the supervisor to prove that fairness obtains in such a situation. In such a subjective evaluation, employees have no satisfactory basis upon which to build their expectations. Uncertainty generates mistrust. The charges of favoritism and discrimination and the inevitable disappointments that ensue have a bad effect on supervisor-employee relationships and overall morale within the organization.

There is no adequate alternative to some uniform method of evaluating employee performance if management wishes to avoid charges of discrimination or arbitrary personnel actions. If the appraisal process is based on pooled judgments periodically reconsidered by supervisors when each employee is compared with every other employee in the same work group or rated against specified standards of performance, the results are certainly better than the individual judgments and hasty opinions that could otherwise be used.

Each organization that maintains a formal process should determine when performance appraisals are to be administered. There should be a definite schedule known to everyone. Ideally, performance appraisals should be conducted frequently enough to allow employees to know that their performance is satisfactory or to correct it before it is too late, if improvement is needed. New employees probably need more frequent appraisals than do long-term employees, but this is a delicate issue, since questions of discrimination are likely to arise if everyone is not treated equally. In most libraries performance during a probationary period determines continuing employment. A performance evaluation always should be conducted at the end of the probationary period, whether it is three months, or six, or a year.

Regular performance evaluations are administered on a recurring cycle, either once a year during the same month, or on the individual's birthday, or more commonly, on the anniversary of the date an employee joined the organization. There are advantages and disadvantages to each of those—if they are spread out on birthdays or anniversaries, more time is allowed for reflection and discussion; if they are grouped together during a short time period, comparisons among employees for merit purposes can be made more accurately. In any case the immediate supervisor is the individual who should evaluate the performance of those working for him or her. That person has both knowledge of the job and its requirements, as well as having had an opportunity to observe the individual in the position. This process is supplemented in some institutions with a peer review and/or the involvement of the personnel office in the actual review. Peer reviews are more common for professional positions, and are most evident in those evaluation processes for promotion and tenure used by higher education institutions where librarians have academic or faculty status. Those who question the extensive investment of time required for such formal appraisal processes neglect to place it in the context of job satisfaction and institutional morale.

Another major challenge is establishing standards of performance against which each employee's work can be judged. Standards of performance should be stated in terms of how well the employee is expected to achieve each of the primary responsibilities listed in the job description. A performance standard is a statement of the conditions that will exist when a job has been done satisfactorily. Standards define such things as how well, how frequently, how soon, how accurately, and how much. This is useful as a quality check for the organization. To set standards, one could take the primary responsibilities included in the job description and with each one state, "I will be completely satisfied with your performance when," that sets the parameters for standards. Standards fall into three categories:

Quality-quantity standards: "How well does the employee perform the various tasks set forth in the job description?" and "How much of each task is actually accomplished?" should be questions in the standard setting process. Others include: "Have the standards been based upon job-related criteria developed through job analysis? Do they reflect job results and can that behavior be observed?"

Desired effect standards: "Is work complete, accurate, and performed on time, benefiting the goals and objectives of the institution and users?" is the primary question. "Are sound data gathered as a basis for judgement and decisions?" must also be answered.

Manner of performance standards: "Is the work accomplished in cooperation with others, without friction?" and "Can the employee adapt to new programs or processes ?" are key questions.

The success of any process is measured in terms of how well the individual being rated accepts the standards and statements which eventually go into the appraisal file. Therefore an environment must be created where defenses are dropped so that performance can be addressed. A simple diagram, shown in Figure 12, illustrates the kind of interaction necessary in this process. Figure 13 lists some of the errors supervisors are prone to make in assessing staff performance. It is important to be aware of these pitfalls to avoid making these errors.

PERFORMANCE SYSTEMS

Methods such as MBO, behavioral systems such as BARS essay appraisal, graphic rating, field review, forced choice rating, paired comparisons, performance factor rating, grouping and ranking,

FIGURE 12 Standard Setting Process

If this person is Below Expectation	Does this person know what is expected? Have standards been negotiated?	NO	Negotiate fair standards of acceptable performance
	YES		
	Does this person realize that there is a performance problem?	NO	Counseling; provide feedback; establish problem exists
	YES		
	Is performance acceptable?	NO	Counseling 2: obtain employee involvement in correcting problem
	YES		
At Expectation	Is this person achieving potential in Job?	NO	Coach the employee
	YES		
Exceeding Expectation	Is this person currently capable of additional challenge and responsibility?	NO	Encourage growth through recognition, praise, and additional challenge in small increments
	YES		
	Is this person prepared for additional challenge and responsibility?	NO	Develop the employee
	YES		Promote or reassign, if possible [2]

proficiency tests, trait-rating scales, critical incidents, and check-lists are all used in business organizations and each has found some nitch in the library community. There is no one ideal standard method of performance appraisal.

Keep in mind that rating scales, forms, and schedules cannot take precedence over individual growth, so that relationship variables like rapport, trust, and goodwill must be developed and maintained. Employees see performance feedback from a manager as meaningful only when that relationship is established. But most performance appraisal systems require the manager to act as judge, to evaluate and to criticize, thus setting up a potentially adversarial role.[3]

The problem with many evaluation instruments is that they are vague, not job specific, lack validity, and rely heavily on traits for evaluation items. Others, although more complicated to administer, are more likely to fulfill the requirements for libraries. Most personnel specialists view the use of objective appraisal criteria as a safer strategy than the use of subjective standards. Several of both types will be discussed here.

Essays and ratings of a general nature: where the rater is asked to conduct an overall performance estimate. This is conducted in essay form, with the general analysis and qualifiers such as "outstanding" indicated at the conclusion. The essay can be unstructured, but the rater usually is asked to respond to general questions relating to the employee's job knowledge, strengths and weaknesses. The length, depth, and content of essays varies with the rater and this is the most cited major disadvantage. Consistency is also difficult to achieve because each rater has a bias toward his or her own interests. Writing style is also an issue which is likely to affect the process. This approach is quite limited because specific performance criteria are missing. It is also a process which is questionable from a legalistic standpoint. If used, it would be most effectively combined with some other techniques.

Graphic rating system: is the most commonly used method of performance appraisal. This is a method in which the evaluator rates the employee on factors such as quantity of work, dependability, initiative, job knowledge, and accuracy. Typically, the factor is listed with a qualifying sentence. The evaluator is then required to indicate the performance by placing a mark on a horizontal line, as shown in Figure 14. Of course it is always difficult to agree on the definition of terms and to apply them consistently. There is always a possibility that they will be inter-

FIGURE 13 Errors of Rating

ERROR	EXPLANATION
Halo Effect	When the supervisor gives a favorable rating to all position responsibilities based on impressive performance in just one of several job functions. Evaluators who make this error are often evaluating the employee in terms of their own personal mental attitude toward the employee rather than by careful attention to the individual factors of the work performance.
Loose Rater Effect	When the supervisor deliberately rates everyone highly, thus avoiding conflict by not pointing out weaknesses. It is not uncommon to find supervisors who tend to give all subordinates relatively high ratings because the supervisor does not want to face unpleasantness. This leniency places all ratings close to the top of the scale, thus rendering the evaluation useless to management and unfair to clearly outstanding employees. This approach can also create an unrealistic feeling of success when in fact improvement in performance may be needed.
Central Tendency Effect	The supervisor rates everyone as average, thereby avoiding making judgements. Although it is expected that on a normal distribution curve more people will be rated closer to the mean than to any other point on the scale, when all ratings are clustered at the center the consequence is that most of the value of the systematic performance appraisal is lost
Pitchfork Effect	The opposite of the halo effect, where the supervisor gives a poor rating to all position responsibilities based on poor performance in only one job function. This error of "prejudice" is one which often borders on constitutional violation

Continued

FIGURE 13 *Continued*

Tight Rater Effect	The supervisor rates everyone poorly because the supervisor feels that no one measures up to the standards which may or may not be stated in writing. Sometimes these raters have artificially high standards which few staff can ever achieve. Taken together, the "Loose Rater and the Tight Rater" create problems because staff who work at the same level of performance will receive vastly different ratings depending upon the supervisor.
Recency Bias Effect	The supervisor places too much reliance on recent events to determine the individual staff member's performance, rather than on the full period under review.
Length of Service Bias Effect	The supervisor automatically assumes that a long time staff member performs well because of their long experience in the library.
Competetive Rater Bias Effect	The supervisor determines a staff member's rating based upon that person's rating that he or she received from his/her own supervisor.
Association Bias Effect	A busy supervisor may rate factors at the same level merely because they follow each other on the page. This often happens when the supervisor is tired or bored or harried and tries to make judgement without facts.
Contract Bias Effect	The supervisor does not measure the work the staff member has actually accomplished but instead measures what he or she thinks the employee has the potential to achieve.[4]

FIGURE 14 Graphic Rating System (Example 1)

<u>Dependable</u> in the timeliness and responsibility of work duties performed.

Poor   Fair   Average   Good   Excellent

——   ——   ——   ——   ——

---

preted differently by different individuals. Another more sophisticated scale would utilize phrases to describe the levels of performance, as shown in Figure 15. Such scales require a bit more time to construct but are standardized, and comparable among individuals. However, they are subject to the errors already mentioned.

Personality based systems: traits perceived as being significant for positions, including: loyalty, initiative, creativity, ingenuity, drive, trustworthiness, intelligence, etc., are factors included in such approaches. Some scales are accompanied by brief explanations. When a form is developed, all of the personality traits perceived to be important in the job are listed. Unfortunately, its greatest drawback is that it is often administered without adequate definition and is open to a subjective review by raters. Trait-rating scales use a numerical, Likert type rating scale (on a scale of 1-10; or sometimes 1-5) utilizing descriptors (poor, below average, average, above average, excellent); raters are asked to indicate the degree to which the individual possess those desired traits. Again, since this approach lacks job-related definitions, they are subject to errors of halo effect, strictness, leniency or central tendency, all of which can skew the evaluation. A "forced-distribution" system, which assumes a normal distribution curve, has been developed to minimize the possibility of clustering. Under such a method, a rater is required to compare the performance of employees and place a certain percentage of employees at various performance intervals, with the very highest and the very lowest in the smallest groups, as illustrated in Figure 16. Such scales are questionable from a legalistic standpoint. They are not only subjective, but also unreliable and of questionable validity. Of all the rating forms, this type is probably the simplest to perform.

Ranking procedures: Where the rater is asked to provide an

FIGURE 15 Graphic Rating System (Example 2)

Makes frequent errors.	Careless, often makes errors.	Usually accurate. Only makes average number of errors.	Requires little supervision. Is exact and precise most of the time.	Requires absolute minimum of supervision. Is almost always accurate.

overall evaluation of performance by checking categories (top 10%; bottom 25%, etc). The simplest system, then, compares and ranks the employees from highest to lowest by comparing two at a time and then inserting others' performance evaluation as they are compared with those individuals just being rated. This process is repeated until all have been ranked. The paired comparison method is an organized way of comparing each employee with every other employee, one at a time. The disadvantages are that it does not reveal the amount of differences between persons in adjacent ranks and the fact that individuals with the same performance rating must be separated, because no two can occupy the same position in the ranking. Again, since they are most often not related to job-related performance, ranking procedures are subject to legal questioning.

Critical incident: requires that the rater document positive and negative behavioral events that have occurred during the given performance period. It requires observation and recording, and therefore produces a feeling of "looking over the shoulder." Sometimes other procedures are used in conjunction with this approach, nevertheless it must be little used in the profession since there are few recorded cases in library literature.

Behavioral description systems: include job description and analysis of performance based upon it. Appraisal measures can be defined by specific, job-related behaviors. These performance appraisal formats present specific behavioral examples for each performance level. They are useful because they detail what is required to perform effectively and reduce bias in ratings. An example is the BARS (Behaviorally Anchored Rating Scales) system. According to some authorities BARS is the most researched and least used management tool in modern management history.

FIGURE 16 Personality Rating System Scale

10%	20%	40%	20%	10%
Lowest	Below Average	Average	Above Average	Best

Nevertheless, it is used and is worth consideration. This is an example of a system based upon job analysis to determine job performance. It was developed to correct some of the deficiencies in graphic rating scales. The BARS system includes specific statements of the behavior requirements for success on the job. Since each job has several dimensions, a separate scale is developed for each one. The "anchors" are specific written descriptions of actual job behaviors that supervisors agree represent specific levels of performance. A supervisor using BARS would scan the list of anchors on each scale until the anchors best describing the employee's job behavior are identified. The scale value opposite those anchors is then checked. A total evaluation is obtained by combining the scale values chosen for each of the job dimensions.

Such ratings are good predictors of success, particularly for lower level jobs and are best used where requirements can be quantified and specific. They are less reliable for professional personnel where independence is needed. BARS tries to relate success to behavior and is derived from critical incidents of effective and ineffective job-related behavior. Emphasis is upon results which come from the development of individuals:

Performance improvement occurs when managers enlist employee support and input into the process. Just as with all effective performance measures, it is time-consuming because each job dimension must be described. Motivation to perform then becomes three pronged: it is the result of a person's expectations as to the relationship between increased effort leading to improved performance; increased performance leading to reward; and the anticipated value of the reward to that person.[6]

FIGURE 17 BARS Scale System

Scale values	Anchors
7 () Excellent	Develops a comprehensive project plan, documents it well, obtains required approval, and distributes the plan to all concerned.
6() Very good	Plans, communicates, and observes milestones; states week by week where the project stands relative to plans. Maintains up-to-date charts of project accomplishments and backlogs and uses these to optimize any schedule modifications required.
	Experiences some minor operational problems, but communicates effectively.
5() Good	Lays out all the parts of a job and schedules each part; seeks to beat schedule and will allow for slack.
	Satisfies customers' time constraints; time and cost overruns occur infrequently.
4() Average	Makes a list of due dates and revises them as the project progresses, usually adding unforeseen events; instigates frequent customer complaints.
	May have a sound plan, but does not keep track of milestones; does not report slippages in schedule or other problems.
3() Below average	Plans are poorly defined, unrealistic time schedules are common.
	Cannot plan more than a day or two ahead, has no concept of a realistic project date.
2() Very poor	Has no plan or schedule of work segments to be performed.
	Does little or no planning for project.
1() Unacceptable	Seldom if ever completes project because of lack of planning and does not care.
	Fails consistently due to lack of planning and does not inquire about how to improve.[5]

These are the first legally defensible measures which have been discussed so far. The process of BARS involves several steps:

- The manager and the job holder, both familiar with the job, identify several activities that are critical to effective performance. These become performance dimensions.
- For each of these dimensions several specific statements are written, based on observations of effective job performance. These statements tell what job incumbents actually do. Similarly, statements are written describing ineffective job performance. Lastly, job actions are noted that reflect neither very effective nor very ineffective performance. Statements that are vague, duplicative, or do not cite observable behavior are eliminated.
- All the statements are fed back to each manager or job holder, who is then asked to assign each statement to the dimension it best fits. Only those statements whose placement is agreed upon by a large majority of participants are retained.
- The manager or job holders are asked to scale these statements numerically from 1-10 (very effective to very ineffective). Any scale ranking of a statement that the majority cannot agree upon is eliminated.

Results-centered systems: the supervisor and employee together establish agreements for a period to be measured. This then becomes the basis for evaluation. Management by Objectives (MBO) is the best example and can be used more effectively at the professional level. In this approach the employee and the employer write the job description together; the employee writes the objectives; both the employee and supervisor reach agreement on those objectives; it is determined how to achieve those objectives; and finally there is a performance evaluation conference. This approach has stood the test of job-relatedness and application when supervisors have been trained in goal setting and review of performance. MBO has long been used as a tool for performance appraisal, principally because of the compelling appeal of its logic. It has been the object of substantial criticism, as well, with respect to its underlying assumptions about motivation, its psychological impact on individuals, and pragmatic issues on such matters as investment in time, paperwork, and participation to complete such a process. The determining factors in the success of MBO appear to be the following: defining clear-cut, reasonably difficult goals; genuine participation in goal setting; adequate feedback on performance; and peer competition. This is but one example of an approach that compares expectations with actual results. Goals are set by supervisor and employee and evaluations based upon achievement of the goals agreed upon. Such approaches require a thorough job analysis, and some analytical skills to be most effective.

Management by Objectives is perhaps the most evident example of participative management because it involves everyone, to an extent, in the management process. It can clarify responsibilities, strengthen planning and control, and establish better relationships between supervisors and other staff members. In this process, at the start of appraisal periods, supervisors and staff members agree upon specific results to be obtained during this period; they establish what is to be done, how long it will take, and who is to do it. The whole process rests upon several premises:

1. Clearly stated objectives. If they are not clear, they should be clarified.
2. A succession of specific objectives. Bench marks must be established to measure progress.
3. Delegation of specific objectives. Certain people should be responsible for accomplishing specific objectives.
4. Freedom to act. Subordinates should be presented objectives and authority and then be charged with accomplishment of those specific objectives.
5. Verifiable results. To achieve objectives, it is best to quantify them. If they are nonquantifiable objectives, they may relate to quantifiable ones. For example, if one wants to reduce absenteeism by 50%, the reasons for absenteeism must be considered. If the reasons relate to morale, then morale must be improved.
6. Clear communication. This exists only when objectives are specific, are agreed upon by all parties, are budgeted, and are known by all individuals who have a reason for knowing.
7. Shared responsibilities. Team effort is the key to Management by Objectives.
8. Personal accountability. Each person must be accountable for the achievement of his or her assigned objectives.
9. Improving management ability. Management is able to plan more objectively when these premises are accepted.

Studies have confirmed that the process does, indeed, improve communications, increase mutual understanding, improve planning, create positive attitudes toward the evaluation process, utilize management abilities, and promote innovation within organizations which have used it.[7]

Competency-based systems: Measures can also be built around competencies—knowledge, skills, abilities, motivation, and other personal characteristics which lead to high performance. They may be characteristics (cooperation, setting priorities, risk-taking) that distinguish between effective and ineffective performers. They must also be well defined in behavioral terms in order to reduce subjectivity in their application. Competency-based performance appraisal systems recognize the importance of how an individual's characteristics influence results obtained. Performance appraisal for professional personnel largely involves compliance with goals, duties, ethics, and standards of conduct as proclaimed by professional associations such as the American Library Association through its *Code of Ethics* and *Library Bill of Rights* statements. As a result, standards reflect an integration of position-specific accountabilities and professional practices. Training and career development seeks to improve professional competence.[8]

In any goal-setting process past performance is evaluated in relation to the achievement of previously agreed upon goals and the employee is informed of how well he or she has performed.

THE CONFERENCE

After the type of review has been selected or developed and the necessary documentation is in place, the next formal step in the review process is to distribute the forms. Usually this is done by the personnel department, but in smaller institutions may be accomplished through the librarian's office. If everyone is being evaluated at the same time, this logistical administrative process is easier. If not, a system of identifying who and when must be instituted. The supervisor of the employee to be reviewed receives the forms first, and that person becomes the rater. It is then that person's responsibility to complete the form and ensure a successful process. Oftentimes notes, taken over a period of time, are helpful in completing the form and preparing for the interview which will follow. This is particularly important if the possibility exists that there will be a negative evaluation. The rater should be objective and aware of the biases already mentioned. But the rater should not be averse to giving negative ratings, where appropriate. An accurate and truthful evaluation enables the individual to grow and the organization to benefit in the long run. In order to ensure objectivity before the process is complete, the rating should be reviewed by the next person in the supervisory hierarchy. Consensus should be reached on the rating before further steps are taken.

The interview or performance discussion is the next step. Whether the meeting is more of an interview or a mutual discussion will depend upon the type of appraisal system used and the extent to which the supervisor involves the employee in performance planning and assessment. The most successful appraisals are those in which the supervisor listens most of the time and is able to build upon that communication technique. To listen nonjudgmentally is not easy, but the alternative is limited feedback, little motivation, no problem identification, and superficial counseling. The meeting should be well structured, nonthreatening and scheduled at a time and place convenient for both parties. Before the interview the employee should be encouraged to prepare for the interview by being requested to think about accomplishments, goals, skills used, and how the supervisor can be helpful in meeting those. This is basically a self-appraisal. The employee should receive a copy of the written appraisal form at least a full working day in advance of the meeting, which allows an opportunity for a review of the evaluation. The written evaluation should have identified both strengths and weaknesses.

In the interview the supervisor should do most of the listening, asking pertinent questions and making enlightened comments to encourage the employee to talk. The discussion should focus on the performance appraisal, with opportunities for the employee to question unclear reasons and to eventually accept the appraisal. The purpose of the process is to help employees become more effective on the job, and to grow in the organization. The best way of effecting an improvement is by listening to why an employee does what he or she does the way it is done. In a nonthreatening atmosphere, all defenses are down so that both parties can deal with actual performance and its success as well as its inadequacies. During the interview a review of the performance goals should be conducted, evaluating accomplishment of the goals for the period just ending. Problems which prevented achievement of any goal should be identified and the supervisor should assess how he or she might be helpful in removing those barriers.

One measure of success is whether the employee agrees that a new way of performing certain tasks might be desirable. Only then

FIGURE 18 Guide to Employee Performance Appraisal

PERFORMANCE FACTORS	OUTSTANDING	ABOVE AVERAGE	AVERAGE	FAIR	POOR
QUALITY	Leaps tall buildings with a single bound	Must take running start to leap over tall buildings	Can leap over short buildings only	Crashes into buildings when attemping to leap over them	Cannot recognize buildings at all
TIMELINESS	Is faster than a speeding bullet	Is as fast as a speeding bullet	Not quite as fast as a speeding bullet	Would you believe a slow bullet	Wounds self with bullets when attempting to shoot
INITIATIVE	Is stronger than a locomotive	Is stronger than a bull elephant	Is stronger than a bull	Shoots the bull	Smells like a bull
ADAPTABILITY	Walks on water consistently	Walks on water in emergencies	Washes with water	Drinks water	Passes water in emergencies
COMMUNICATION	Talks with God	Talks with the Angels	Talks to himself	Argues with himself	Loses arguments with himself

Source unknown

can goals and objectives for the next review period be established. These should always be action goals which reflect results to be achieved, not simply an activity. The final step in that process is for the employee and supervisor to sign the evaluation form, thereby accepting the evaluation and proposed future directions. After the interview the employee should be able to answer these questions: How am I doing? Where do I need improvement? How do I achieve that? Will I receive help? What have I really accomplished? In what ways do I contribute to the success of this library? How can my supervisor help me in that achievement? At the conclusion there should be a restatement of what has been mutually agreed upon. The whole process must be conducted in a manner that protects the individual's right to privacy. Also an appeals process must be in place, should the employee contest an evaluation.

To reiterate, the four most important components of this process are:

- The job description, upon which standards can be established by enumerating what is expected;
- The written performance standards, upon which performance appraisal can be conducted by determining how well employees are expected to perform;
- The performance appraisal, upon which future goals and objectives can be set and which has provided feedback on performance; and
- The performance goals and objectives themselves.

Every assurance should be given that there will be follow-through, otherwise the process becomes a useless exercise and the employee becomes disillusioned. For examples of performance assessment forms, see Appendix III.

As a final comment on this serious topic, Figure 18 is offered as comic relief.

REFERENCES

1. G.V. Barrett and M.C. Kernan, "Performance Appraisal and Terminations," *Personnel Psychology*, v. 40 (Autumn 1987):501.

2. Neil A. Stroul, "Whither Performance Appraisal?" *Training and Development Journal*, v. 41 (Nov. 1987):70.

3. *Ibid.*

4. T. R. Lowe, "Eight Ways to Ruin Performance Reviews," *Personnel Journal,* v. 65 (Jan. 1986):60-62.

5. C. E. Schneier and R. W. Beatty, "Developing Behaviorally Anchored Rating Scales (BARS)," *Personnel Administrator,* (Aug., 1979):12.

6. William J. Kearney, "Behaviorally Anchored Rating Scales—MBO's Missing Ingredient," *Personnel Journal,* v. 57 (Jan. 1979):22.

7. Stephen J. Carroll, Jr. and Henry L. Tosi, Jr., *Management by Objectives.* New York: Macmillan, 1973, p. 3.

8. David L. Devries, et. al., *Performance Appraisal on the Line.* New York: John Wiley & Sons, 1981, p. 38.

SELECTED BIBLIOGRAPHY

Abella, Kay Tyler. *Building Successful Training Programs: A Step-by-Step Guide.* Reading, MA: Addison-Wesley, 1986.

Anthony, William F. *Managing Incompetence.* New York: AMACOM, 1981.

Bowes, Lee. *No One Need Apply: Getting and Keeping the Best Workers.* Boston: Harvard Business School Press, 1987.

Conroy, Barbara. *Learning Packaged to Go: Directory and Guide to Staff Development and Training Packages.* Phoenix, AZ: Oryx Press, 1983.

————. *Library Staff Development and Continuing Education: Principles and Practices.* Littleton, CO: Libraries Unlimited, 1983.

Cottam, Keith M., ed. *Employee Selection and Minimum Qualifications for Librarians.* Chicago: American Library Association, 1984. (OLPR T.I.P. (Topics in Personnel) Kit #6).

Creth, Sheila D. *Effective On-The-Job Training.* Chicago: American Library Association, 1986.

———— and Frederick Duda, eds. *Personnel Administration in Libraries,* 2nd ed. New York: Neal-Schuman Publishers, 1989.

Devries, David L., et. al. *Performance Appraisal on the Line.* New York: John Wiley & Sons, 1981.

Dewey, Barbara I. *Library Jobs: How to Fill Them, How to Find Them.* Phoenix: Oryx Press, 1987.

Guy, Jeniece, ed. *Writing Library Job Descriptions.* Chicago: American Library Association, 1985. (OLPR T.I.P. Kit #7).

King, Geraldine, ed. *Managing Employee Performance.* Chicago: American Library Association, 1985. (OLPR Spec Kit #11).

King, Patricia. *Performance Planning & Appraisal: A How-To Book for Managers.* New York: McGraw-Hill Book Company, 1989.

Lipow, Anne G., ed. *Staff Development: A Practical Guide.* Chicago: American Library Association, LAMA, 1988.

McQuaig, Jack H., et. al. *How to Interview and Hire Productive People.* New York: Frederick Fell Publishers, 1981.

Odiorne, George S. *Strategic Management of Human Resources: A Portfolio Approach.* San Francisco: Jossey-Bass Publishers, 1984.

Olson, Richard F. *Performance Appraisal: A Guide to Greater Productivity.* New York: John Wiley & Sons, 1981.

Scholick, Gary P. *Interview Guide for Supervisors.* 3rd ed. Washington, D.C.: College and University Personnel Associations, 1988.

APPENDIX I

JOB DESCRIPTIONS

TEAM LEADER, Arabic Team, Processing Services Department, Sterling Memorial
 Library
Minimum rank: Librarian II

THE UNIVERSITY AND THE LIBRARY

Yale University is one of the foremost universities of the world, preeminent in
scholarship and research in the various fields of the humanities, the sciences,
the social sciences, and in the professional schools. Twelve schools or
colleges offer courses of study: Yale College, Graduate School, School of
Medicine, Divinity School, Law School, School of Art, School of Architecture,
School of Music, School of Forestry and Environmental Sciences, School of
Nursing, School of Drama, and School of Organization and Management. The
University Library has 8.9 million volumes housed in the Sterling Memorial
Library, 16 school and department libraries and numerous distinguished special
collections. The Processing Services Department, which serves as the central
cataloging agency for the Library, includes a staff of approximately 100.

RESPONSIBILITIES

Under the general direction of the Head, Processing Services Department,
manages the full range of work activities in processing and cataloging
monographs and serials in Arabic and other Near Eastern languages. Assists in
collection development activities for Arabic materials. Develops effective
working relationships with faculty in this subject area and may be called upon
to provide reference assistance from time to time. Responsible for the
organization of materials in the Unit. Recommends policies and establishes
procedures for the work of the Unit. Creates original cataloging records for
monographs and serials; prepares full descriptive cataloging records according
to national standards; assigns subject headings according to local practice.
Establishes and revises name headings according to national cataloging
standards. Prepares name authority records for Yale catalogs; may prepare name
authority records for shared authority file with Library of Congress and/or
other authority work and classification; resolves cataloging problems. Keeps
abreast of revisions in cataloging rules and trends and applies new rules and
interpretations as appropriate. Supervises the work of cataloging assistants.
Participates in the Library's planning activities and is expected to be active
professionally.

TEAM LEADER, Arabic Team, continued . . .

QUALIFICATIONS

MLS from an ALA-accredited library school. A minimum of two years of library experience at the professional level required. Strong knowledge of Arabic. Previous cataloging experience. Demonstrated ability to work effectively with faculty, students, administrators, and library colleagues. Knowledge of current cataloging code; Library of Congress subject heading and classification practices. Educational background in Arabic and/or Islamic Studies. Supervisory experience; familiarity with Library of Congress rule interpretations; familiarity with MARC format and content designation; reading knowledge of other Near Eastern languages, especially Persian and Turkish, preferred.

SALARY AND BENEFITS

Salary and rank dependent upon qualifications and experience; from a minimum of $27,300. Comprehensive benefits program including 22 vacation days, 17 holiday, recess and personal days, health care, retirement plan, and relocation assistance.

Applications received by April 13, 1990 will be given first consideration; applications will be accepted until the position is filled. Please send letter of application, resume, and the names of three references to Diane Y. Turner, Acting Head, Library Personnel Services, Yale University Library, Post Office Box 1603A Yale Station, New Haven, Connecticut 06520. Yale is an equal opportunity affirmative action employer.

ARIZONA STATE UNIVERSITY LIBRARIES

JOB DESCRIPTION

TITLE: Circulation/Reserve Unit Head, Access Services Department

CLASSIFICATION: Library Assistant IV (Grade 14)

PRIME FUNCTION:

Under the direction of the Head of Access Services, supervises the Circulation and Reserve Units of that department. Independently makes decisions on issues affecting daily routine, manages staff of lesser classification including part-time workers, and insures the smooth operation of the units. Performs all duties associated with the circulation of library materials and the provision of Reserve materials. Responsible for routine maintenance activities associated with the online circulation and reserve system, including daily interface with Systems Support staff.

DUTIES AND RESPONSIBILITIES:

1.   Manages the activities of the units, including setting workflow priorities, seeing that appropriate procedures and policies are followed and work is accomplished.

2.   Hires, trains, supervises, evaluates and schedules unit staff both full-time and part-time. At present, the full-time staff in Circulation consists of a Library Assistant II (night supervisor), a Library Assistant I (book return/weekend supervisor), two Clerk II's (holds and searches). The part-time staff consists of 10 to 15 workers, both student and Clerk I's. In Reserve, the staff consists of 2.5 Clerk II's as well as student employees.

3.   Coordinates the Circulation Unit's interface with other Access Services units and other library departments.

4.   Assumes responsibility for routine maintenance activities associated with the online circulation system, keeping Systems Support staff informed of equipment problems and production errors.

5.   Prepares statistical reports.

6.   Manages units' wage budgets.

7.   Provides loan policy, directional and referral information in response to patron questions.

8.   Checks out and returns materials at the Circulation and Reserve desks, processing materials to meet system specifications.

9.   Assists patrons in filling out various library forms, including but not limited to search cards, hold cards, applications for courtesy cards,

and Reserve requests.

10. Screens and/or handles patron complaints, referring same to Billing Unit Head or Access Services department head.

11. Responsible for scheduling staff at the Circulation Desk and Reserve Counter.

12. Maintains overall responsibility for opening and closing the library.

13. Occasionally performs various tasks associated with circulation, including but not limited to holds, searches, issuance of courtesy cards, telephone renewal and preliminary billing tasks.

14. Occasionally performs various tasks associated with Reserve, including but not limited to processing materials for Reserve, taking materials off Reserve, circulation of Reserve material and billing.

15. Performs other duties as assigned.

QUALIFICATIONS:

Required:

- Five years of library experience, OR
- A Bachelor's degree with Library Science coursework and one year library experience, OR
- Any equivalent combination of experience, training and/or education approved by the Personnel Department.
- Considerable knowledge of library operations and procedures;
- Demonstrated supervisory ability;
- Ability to exercise judgment and initiative;
- Ability to deal effectively and tactfully with the public, peers and subordinates.
- Public service experience.

Preferred:

- Academic library experience, preferably in circulation working with an automated system.
- Successful supervisory experience.
- Knowledge of Reserve procedures.

Anticipated Work Schedule:

Monday-Friday, 8:00 a.m. - 5:00 p.m., plus occasional evenings, weekends and/or holidays.

EMPLOYEE   SUPERVISOR   DATE

AURORA PUBLIC SCHOOLS

Job Description

TITLE: School Media Specialist

REPORTS TO: Immediate Supervisor -
                    Building Principal

INDIVIDUALS
SUPERVISED: Under direction of the Principal -
                    Media aide or media clerks as assigned to the media center and
                    media center volunteers

JOB SUMMARY: The media specialist shall work under the direction of the principal
                    and within the parameters of the District goals, objectives and
                    program, and in cooperation with the Director of Media Services.
                    The media specialist demonstrates an in-depth knowledge of the
                    media area and its relationship to other programs and the skills to
                    work cooperatively with staff to plan, develop and implement the
                    program. The media specialist shall provide leadership in evaluation
                    and selection of media print and non-print materials and shall be
                    responsible for their circulation. The media specialist shall work
                    with and through other teachers for the benefit of students, and to
                    promote the effective use of media materials and equipment.

MAJOR DUTIES: 1. Participates with the principal to coordinate media support for
                        the curricular program.
                    2. Works cooperatively with teachers in the design and prepara-
                        tion of units of study.
                    3. Exercises a leadership role in encouraging media utilization by
                        students and staff.
                    4. Coordinates the implementation of the Aurora Public Schools
                        Media Skills Guideline program.
                    5. Cooperates in the facilitation of student learning activities
                        which may be done in the classroom as well as in the media
                        center to meet a variety of student needs, interest and
                        abilities.
                    6. Assists students in selection of materials and equipment and
                        advises teachers about new and existing materials and
                        techniques.
                    7. Provides reference assistance and education to students and
                        staff.
                    8. Participates with the principal in developing a system to
                        provide regular communication about media services and
                        program with staff, students and parents.
                    9. Develops, in consultation with the principal and staff, a plan
                        and priorities for media center services and operation.
                    10. Recommends, in cooperation with the faculty and under the
                        direction of the principal, an annual budget for media
                        materials, equipment and services based on District and
                        building goals; coordinates requisitions for such media
                        materials, equipment and services and maintains an accurate
                        record of expenditures.

11. Participates in the recommendation of media clerks, aides, volunteers and student assistants when practical. Coordinates the training and duties of those assigned to the media center.
12. Compiles and maintains records of media materials, equipment and services as needed for evaluation and reporting to appropriate agencies.
13. Coordinates procedures for selection, processing and cataloging media materials and equipment according to District guidelines, and provides for arranging and circulating these materials and equipment for effective utilization in the instructional program.
14. Maintains the building collection of materials and equipment in good condition through inventory, weeding and repairing, and utilizing recognized techniques for collection development such as collection mapping.
15. Provided inservice as needed in use of media equipment for faculty and students, and production and development of media materials.
16. Coordinates media technology and available production facilities and services to support the instructional program.
17. Pursues professional growth activities in order to keep abreast of new information and development in the field of media.
18. Participates as assigned with the District curriculum committees concerned with the design and development of curricular programs.
19. Consults with administration and faculty on effective use of space and furnishings in the media center to provide a positive and inviting atmosphere conducive to learning.
20. Performs other duties as assigned.

L02093

<u>Cataloging Assistant III</u> (Level C)
Processing Services/Arabic Team

Normal Work Schedule: Monday – Friday, 8:30 – 5:00 p.m.;
                               37.5 hours per week

Under the general guidance of the Arabic Team Leader, performs a variety of
processing activities for library materials in Arabic and other Middle Eastern
Languages, using Library of Congress (LC) and Research Libraries Group (RLG)
member bibliographic records. After initial training period, must be able to
apply knowledge of bibliographic and acquisitions elements significant in
machine readable processing, local processing conventions, CRT operation, and
organization of the card catalog.

1. Verifies descriptive elements of LC and RLG member source copy with
    book in hand and makes appropriate changes to cataloging copy as
    specified in guidelines. Completes or modifies LC cataloging-in-
    process (CIP) copy.
2. Changes call number as necessary to conform to Yale practice.
3. Adds information to RLIN data base and to local catalogs (including an
    online catalog; edits cataloging records, providing appropriate tags
    according to MARC format and the requirements of the online
    bibliographic data system. Performs other data base activities as
    required.
4. Transfers and reclassifies previously cataloged titles following
    Processing Services Department procedures.
5. Searches printed catalogs and computerized data base for LC and RLG
    member copy.
6. Adds and replaces copies.
7. Sorts, verifies, shelves, retrieves, and otherwise processed
    acquisitions, in-process, and backlog material.
8. May file catalog cards.
9. May prepare authority records for local catalogs as necessary.
10. Performs other related duties as required.

QUALIFICATIONS

Required:

1. Four years of related work experience, two of them in the same job
    family at the next lower level, and a high school level education; or
    two years of related work experience and an Associate degree; or an
    equivalent combination of experience and education.
2. Minimal keyboarding skills.
3. Good reading knowledge of Arabic.
4. Previous work experience must demonstrate accuracy, consistency, and
    dependability in performing work assignments and in following detailed
    procedures.

Page 2.

L02093

<u>Cataloging Assistant III</u> (Level C)
Processing Services/Arabic Team

Normal Work Schedule: Monday – Friday, 8:30 – 5:00 p.m.;
                        37.5 hours per week

Preferred:

1. Experience in the use of RLIN, OCLC, NOTIS, or comparable system.

APPENDIX II

RECRUITMENT AND INTERVIEW FORMS

YALE UNIVERSITY LIBRARY

RECRUITMENT PLAN AND SCHEDULE

M & P / Librarian Positions

Position Title:_____ Req.# _____

Department/Unit:_____ Min. Libn. Rank _____

Former Incumbent:_____ M & P Grade _____

Date Available: _____ Salary Min. _____

Hiring Supervisor: _____

Applications to: _____

Application deadline: _____

Anticipated appointment date of new hire _____

University Posting Date _____ Library Posting Date _____

Advertisements:

_____ C R L NEW   Issue _____ Sent _____
         (due 2nd of preceding month)

_____ Chronical Higher Ed   Issue _____ Sent _____

_____ American Libraries   Issue _____ Sent _____
         (due 5th of preceding month)

_____ Local newspaper(s)   (specify) _____

_____ Other _____   Issue _____ Sent _____

Special Mailing to:

_____ ARL Directors
_____ ARL Personnel Officers
_____ ALA-Accredited Library School Placement Offices
_____ Minority Recruitment   Source:_____
_____ Other, specify:

_____   _____
Signature of Library Personnel officer Date

```
                         YALE UNIVERSITY
             OFFICE OF LIBRARY PERSONNEL SERVICES
         GUIDELINES FOR CANDIDATES INVITED TO BE INTERVIEWED
```

The following guidelines have been developed to help you in planning your trip to New Haven. On the morning of your interview, you will be given an expense report form to sign. This will be used to request your reimbursement once you have submitted your receipts. If you have any questions, please feel free to call Christine Pedevillano at 203/432-1810.

1. Please make your own travel arrangements. When making airline reservations, please make an effort to get the lowest airfare available. Save your ticket receipts and submit them for reimbursement.

2. You will be reimbursed for airport or train station parking.

3. Keep track of any mileage for your private automobile. Yale will reimburse at the rate of .21 per mile. Where possible ask for toll and bridge receipts.

4. Where possible, get receipts for taxis, otherwise itemize. In case you cannot remember the amount paid, we do know approximate fares from the local airport, train or limo station to the hotel.

5. A hotel reservation for a single room will be made in your name and billed directly to Yale. If you are traveling with another person, you are expected to pay the difference between single and double occupancy, unless prior arrangements and approval have been given.

6. A hotel reservation is only made for the evening before the interview unless other arrangements have been made through our office prior to your visit.

7. Yale will not reimburse for any long distance telephone calls made from your hotel room. Guests are expected to make payment at the desk when checking out for any telephone charges other than local calls.

8. Yale will not reimburse for various charges such as laundry bills, or other services provided by the hotel. Any other charges or reimbursements that are not outlined in thes guidelines must have prior approval from our office.

9. Yale cannot extend services such as tickets to university sporting events or gymnasium privileges.

10. Please outline and submit your receipts no later than 2 weeks after your interview for prompt reimbursement.

Library Personnel; 2/2/88

Yale University

Library Personnel Office
P.O. Box 1603A Yale Station
New Haven, Connecticut 06520-7429

Campus address:
Sterling Memorial Library
120 High Street
Telephone:
203 432-1810

Date

NAME
ADDRESS

Dear _____:

I am pleased to confirm the arrangements for your interview on July 1, 1988 for the position of Head, Science Libraries at Yale University. As we discussed, a double reservation has been made in your name at the Colony Inn for the evening of June 30. Please plan to meet Millicent D. Abell, University Librarian, and Jack A. Siggins, Deputy University Librarian in the lobby of the hotel at 7:00 p.m. that evening. Reservations for dinner will have been arranged at an area restaurant.

I have enclosed your interview schedule for the day and other materials which will help to acquaint you with the library system. Please be sure to ask at the hotel desk in the event that other materials have been left for you.

We will reimburse your travel and meal expenses as soon as possible after you have submitted your receipts. If you have any questions, please do not hesitate to call me at the office at 203/432-1810.

We look forward to meeting you.

Sincerely,

Christine Pedevillano
Personnel Representative

YALE UNIVERSITY LIBRARY

Interview Schedule
for

NAME

Candidate, Head, Science Libraries
Kline Science Library

Friday, July 1, 1988

JUNE 30, 1988

7:00 P.M.	Colony Inn Lobby 1157 Chapel Street	Meet Millicent D. Abell and Jack A. Siggins for dinner

---

8:30 a.m.	Library Personnel Services Sterling Memorial Library Room 117B	Meet with Maureen Sullivan, Head, Library Personnel Services
9:00 a.m.	Office of the Associate University Librarian for Collection Development Sterling Memorial Library	Meet with Karin Trainer, Associate University Librarian; and Michael Keller, Associate University Librarian for Collection Development
10:00 a.m.	Librarian's Office Sterling Memorial Library Room 152	Meet with Jack A. Siggins, Deputy University Librarian
12 noon	Mory's	Lunch with Maureen Sullivan and other Science librarians
1:45 p.m.	Kline Science Library	Meet with Jack A. Siggins, Deputy University Librarian, and members of the Science Faculty
3:00 p.m.	Conference Room 411 Sterling Memorial Library	Meet with librarians from within the library system
4:00 p.m.	Librarian's Office Sterling Memorial Library Room 152	Meet with Millicent D. Abell, University Librarian
4:45 p.m.	Library Personnel Services Sterling Memorial Library Room 117B	Meet with Maureen Sullivan

YALE UNIVERSITY LIBRARY * * * PRE-EMPLOYMENT REFERENCE CHECK

APPLICANT:_____ DATE:_____

CANDIDATE FOR:_____

Provide a brief description of position (Ascertain whether applicant would have problem(s) with a position of this type):

_____

_____

PREVIOUS OR CURRENT POSITION:_____

Company's Name:_____

Supervisor:_____

Job Title:_____

Dates of employment: From_____ to_____

Reason for leaving:_____

APPLICANT'S RESPONSIBILITIES (IN ORDER OF IMPORTANCE):

_____

_____

_____

STRENGTHS & WEAKNESSES:

_____

_____

COMMENT ON:

Quality of work:_____

Quantity of work:_____

Attendance:_____

Initiative:_____

Co-operativeness/Attitude:_____

Compatibility:_____

Ability to accept criticism:_____

WOULD YOU RE-EMPLOY? yes____ no____ If no, why not?_____

_____

OTHER INFORMATION YOU WOULD LIKE TO PROVIDE:_____

_____

Signature: _____ Date:_____ Title:_____

11/25/85

Yale University

Library Personnel Office
P.O. Box 1603A Yale Station
New Haven, Connecticut 06520-7429

Campus address:
Sterling Memorial Library
120 High Street
Telephone:
203 432-1810

DATE

NAME
ADDRESS

Dear _____ :

    I am delighted to offer you the position of Head, Science Libraries at Yale University. This appointment will be at the rank of Librarian __, with an initial salary of $_____ per year, effective _____.

    Please confirm your acceptance in writing to Maureen Sullivan. If you have any questions or needs, please let us know.

    We are looking forward to working with you.

                    Sincerely,

                    Jack A. Siggins

JAS/cp

cc: Maureen Sullivan - for Personnel File

Yale University

Library Personnel Office
P.O. Box 1603A Yale Station
New Haven, Connecticut 06520-7429

Campus address:
Sterling Memorial Library
120 High Street
Telephone:
203 432-1810

DATE

NAME
ADDRESS

Dear _____:

    We have completed our search for the position of Head, Science Libraries and have appointed Katherine Branch to the position, effective October 1, 1988. Ms. Branch is currently Head of Reference and Circulation in the Welsh Medical Library at Johns Hopkins University. We appreciate your interest in this position in the Yale University Library system.

                           Sincerely,

                           Christine Pedevillano
                           Personnel Representative

CP/ew

Indiana State University Libraries
July 1989

STAFF DEVELOPMENT

The mission of Indiana State University Libraries is to provide information to support the educational, research, recreation, and service needs of the faculty, administration, students, and staff. The Libraries recognize also their responsibility to provide library resources to members of the local community, the citizens of the state, and scholars from around the state and nation. Because the success of this enterprise rests ultimately on the effectiveness of library faculty and staff, it is important that each member have the skills, knowledge, and commitment necessary to provide appropriate levels of service. Staff development activities are, therefore, an essential adjunct to this mission. The library administration strongly supports these activities and considers them an integral part of the overall library program.

Each library staff member shares responsibility for taking advantage of these opportunities, for monitoring his/her own development, for encouraging each other, and for making developmental needs known. The responsibility for providing opportunities for staff development rests most heavily on library administration, supervisors, and the Staff Development Committee. Basically, this requires (1) that opportunities are provided to meet developmental needs, (2) that staff members are informed of opportunities, (3) that appropriate staff members are strongly encouraged to take advantage of opportunities, and (4) that, through library policies and guidelines and a positive managerial attitude, an atmosphere is created and maintained in which the development of individual potential can thrive.

DEFINITION

"Staff development" includes a broad range of activities that addresses developmental needs of support and professional staff, which are (1) position-related, (2) career-related, and (3) quality of life or personal enrichment related. The first two are a concern of the library administration. The third is primarily the individual's personal responsibility and as such is only supported by schedule adjustments pursuant to departmental needs. Staff development is a continual process that orients, trains, and develops each member of the library organization.

STAFF DEVELOPMENT COMMITTEE

The Staff Development Committee is a Library committee, reporting to the Dean of Library Services, composed of five members each appointed for a two-year term. (During the first year one member from each category will be appointed for a one- year term.)

The Dean of Libraries will request the Library Faculty Assembly to recommend five library faculty members from which he will select three members: one from Public Services, one from Technical Services, and one member from the faculty at large. The Dean of Libraries will request the Library Support Staff Representatives to recommend four support staff members from which he will select two.

RESPONSIBILITIES/DUTIES

Responsibility for the implementation and success for the program is shared:

1. **Library Administration**

   a. Planning, coordination, and evaluation of the program.
   b. Implementing orientation program for new employees.
   c. Reviewing and allocating of funds and resources to support staff
      development activities.

2. **Staff Development Committee**

   a. Advises the Library administration on the planning, coordination, and evaluation
      of the Staff Development Program.
   b. Semi-annually conducts a survey of the staff's developmental interests.
   c. Organizes and publicizes programs of interest to the Library staff.
   d. Conducts an evaluation of each program.
   e. Evaluates the Staff Development Program and activities annually and reports the
      results to the Dean and *CML Bulletin*.
   f. Reviews the committee's funding and makes recommendations to the Dean.

g. Periodically announces the receipt of appropriate staff development materials in
 CML Announcements

h. Provides for the recording of selected programs for those unable to attend.
 Recordings will be made available in Teaching Materials, Microforms & Media
 Department for roughly one month.

3. **Library Department and Unit Heads** are responsible for training staff to meet their
 job responsibilities. This must also include:

a. Encouraging staff participation in staff development activities that support the staff
 member's and department's goals.

b. Advising individual staff members on career goals and directions and or referring
 individuals to appropriate counseling services.

c. Interpreting staff development policies.

d. Promoting employee training and development.

e. Routing appropriate staff development information opportunities

4. **Supervisors** act as information links between staff and Department Heads
 regarding the staff development needs and goals of their units. They foster staff
 development within the constraints imposed by the need to accomplish unit goals.

5. **All Library Staff Members** have the responsibility for monitoring their own growth
 and development and alerting their supervisors to specific training and development
 opportunities.

METHODS FOR SUPPORTING STAFF DEVELOPMENT

1. Support for **Library faculty** development will vary depending on funds available,
 scheduling constraints, and the form of staff development, but will generally
 include:

a. Schedule adjustments or release time.

b. Research support (mail, computer support, photocopying, database
 searching, library facilities, staff support, etc.)

c. Release time for research.

d. Paid time (time to attend conferences, meetings, courses, workshops, etc.)

e. Financial reimbursement (to cover travel expenses, registration expenses, etc.)

 f. Sabbatical leaves.

2. Support for **Library support staff** development will depend on funds available,
 scheduling constraints, and form of staff development, but will generally include:

a. Schedule adjustments or release time.

b. Paid time (time to attend seminars, workshops, etc.)

c. Financial reimbursement (to cover travel expenses, registration expenses, etc.)

STAFF DEVELOPMENT ACTIVITIES

This list is not in priority order and is not intended to be comprehensive. The intent of the list is only to provide a sample of staff development activities.

Workshops/Seminars/Institutes (job skills, library skills, new technology, personal development, career development, etc.)
>> local
>> state
>> regional
>> national
>> international

Academic Course Work (job skills, library skills, new technology, personal development, career development, etc.)
>> neighboring institutions

Conference Attendance
>> state
>> regional
>> national
>> international

Research/Publication

Orientation to the Work Unit, Library and Organization
>> new employee orientation program
>> mentoring
>> handbooks, manuals
>> informational meetings/seminars
>> tour of library departments and campus
>> job descriptions

On-the-Job Training
>> manual of job procedures
>> individual skills training, coaching by supervisor
>> instruction and assistance from co-workers and other colleagues
>> class sessions

Career Counseling/Planning/Mentoring

Job Rotation

Staff Exchange

Reading Periodicals/Books

Retreats

Special Assignments

Task Force/Committee Assignments
library
campus
state
regional
national
international

APPENDIX III

PERFORMANCE
EVALUATION FORMS

SIMMONS COLLEGE

Process for Annual Performance Appraisals

The annual performance appraisal provides an opportunity for supervisors and employees to discuss job-related tasks, accomplishments, goals, skills and performance. It is also a time to suggest areas for training and improvement. The review is maintained in the employee's personnel file and may provide the basis for future decisions, including promotions, transfers, or salary increases.

During the performance appraisal interview the supervisor and the employee may share ideas for improving office efficiency and service to students. The supervisor should also ask how s/he might be helpful to the staff member in facilitating the work of the office.

The appraisal consists of the following steps:

1. The supervisor and employee complete the appropriate forms:
   Supervisor: Supervisor's Appraisal of (name of employee)
   Employee: Employee's Self-Appraisal

2. Once the forms are completed, a time is scheduled to discuss the contents of the performance appraisal. It is important to allow for enough time to have a thorough discussion.

3. The discussion may include a free exchange of all aspects of job performance, including job responsibilities, skills, accomplishments, interpersonal skills, understanding of departmental and College mission, and future goals. The discussion should be honest and constructive, and build a strong, supportive relationship between the staff member and the supervisor.

4. After the discussion, a post-interview form (Summary of Supervisor/Employee Performance Appraisal) is completed by the supervisor and signed by the supervisor and employee.

5. The completed form (Summary) is returned to the Director of Human Resources and kept in the employee's confidential file. It will be removed only in specific circumstances - for example, during consideration for a promotion, job transfer, salary increase or if there is difficulty between the employee and the supervisor and one of them asks the Director of Human Resources for help.

6. If there is a disagreement between the supervisor and the employee about the content of the performance appraisal, the supervisor and/or employee should meet with the appropriate Dean or Director of the area. If there continues to be a problem, the supervisor and/or employee may contact the Director of Human Resources.

Tips for Employees:

1. Before your performance appraisal interview, complete the appropriate form and consider the following as you prepare your comments:

a. Make a list of your contributions and achievements during the past year. List training sessions attended and courses taken for professional development.
b. Set short-term and long-range goals for your job. Where are you now? What do you want to accomplish in the next year?
c. Think of things you can do to improve your job performance.

2. At the interview,

a. Listen carefully to the comments and responses of your supervisor during the interview. Clarify anything that is unclear, and summarize what you hear.
b. Be sure your supervisor understands what you are saying. Repeat your points if necessary.
c. Correct any false impressions or incorrect information your supervisor might have about your job performance and accomplishments.
d. If your supervisor outlines areas for improvement, be sure you understand what needs to be improved, how long you have to improve, and what will happen if you don't.
e. Ask your supervisor for an additional session at a future date to discuss progress toward improvement if problem areas are raised in the performance appraisal. This interview should be recorded and included in your personnel file.

Tips for Supervisors:

1. A formal Performance Appraisal is done annually. It follows a series of meetings and discussions throughout the previous year between the employee and the supervisor. Supervisors should schedule regular times throughout the year to discuss office issues and employees' performance.

2. Make sure to provide plenty of time for sharing thoughts, goals, and strategies. Avoid distractions and give full attention to the purpose of the interview.

3. Listen carefully to the responses and comments of the staff member. Clarify and discuss and misunderstandings about performance or job responsibilities.

4. Encourage the staff member to share ways in which you can be helpful to his/her success.

5. After the interview, the staff member should have a clear idea about the necessary areas of improvement, how to improve, and how the supervisor will be of assistance. Staff training sessions, articles, and books, can be suggested.

6. The staff member should have a clear understanding of what will happen if improvement does not occur, and the supervisor should understand the goals of the staff member. Specific goals and a plan of action should be discussed and recorded.

7. If problem areas are discussed, make sure to schedule another session to review the employee's progress toward improvement. Keep communications going.

GUIDELINES FOR DISCUSSION

The following are some of the areas you may wish to include in your discussion(s). Not all elements will apply to all positions. Employees or supervisors who wish to discuss any issues should feel free to contact the Human Resources Office.

PERFORMANCE/WORK HABITS/RESULTS

Attendance, Punctuality: Conforms to scheduled work days/hours.
Communication (Written & Oral): Communicates effectively for the needs of the position, takes pride in final product.
Knowledge of Job: Understands job responsibilities and related tasks; quickly grasps instructions and assignments.
Work Quality: Consistently accurate and thorough; maintains high standards for his/her work; follows through to completion all tasks assigned.
Technical Skills Required to Do The Job: Understands the skills needed to complete the job; demonstrates competence in using specialized knowledge, appropriate office computer software/hardware, institutional equipment.
Planning, Organizational Skills, Setting Priorities: Analyzes and organizes work clearly and intelligently; uses effective work methods; allocates time and determines priorities properly.
Takes Direction, Responds to Supervision: Listens carefully and readily accepts direction and supervision,
Leadership Skills, Teaching Ability: Initiates projects, gains cooperation and confidence of others; delegates authority; explains concepts well; solves problems and intervenes in crisis situations when needed.
Demeanor, Professional Attitude: Cooperativeness and commitment to organizational goals; work accomplished in cooperation with others.
Discretion/Confidential Issues: Maintains confidentiality, tact and good judgment in handling confidential information.
Judgment, Problem Solving: Makes sound, balanced decisions within scope of his/her responsibilities.
Seeks Additional Responsibilities: Accepts responsibility and seeks additional duties.

PERSONAL/INTERPERSONAL

Learning Attitude/Accepts Criticism: Accepts criticism as a means for growth and acts upon it. Learns from mistakes. Welcomes opportunities for growth and development.
Enthusiasm, Energy Level: Demonstrates a commitment to doing the best job possible, attitude contributes to positive staff relationships.
Interpersonal Skills: Is sensitive to feelings of others; deals well and courteously with public and other departments of the College.
Ability to Handle Pressure: Maintains even temperament; reacts calmly and constructively to problems.
Initiative, Ingenuity: Completes tasks without being reminded; is diligent in pursuing new and different situations.
Creativity, Resourcefulness: Is imaginative; copes well with unexpected situations; finds new ways of attacking problems.

SENSE OF COMMUNITY

Mission of the College/Department: Understands the mission of the College and the specific mission of the department.
Flexibility/Cooperativeness: Adapts to new ways of accomplishing tasks; works well as a member of a team; interacts well with people; helps to make things run smoothly.
Ability To See Impact of Function On Other Departments: Sees job as part of the "bigger picture". Is aware of impact of job on other offices and departments as well as to the overall purpose of the College.

SIMMONS COLLEGE
EMPLOYEES'S SELF-APPRAISAL
(For Discussion Purposes)

1. Comment on what you see as your accomplishments this past year, both to your department and to the College. (Consider attitude, performance, and other items listed on the attached sheet of guidelines.)

2. What goals for improvement would you like to set for yourself for the coming year?

3. How can your supervisor be helpful to you in setting and achieving your goals?

4. Are there skills or area of job and staff development that would be helpful to you in your position?

SIMMONS COLLEGE
PERFORMANCE APPRAISAL

DATE_____

EMPLOYEE'S NAME_____ TITLE_____

DEPARTMENT_____

REPORTS TO_____SUPERVISED BY_____

DATE BEGAN WORK_____

DATE OF NEW EMPLOYEE 3-MONTH PERFORMANCE APPRAISAL (if applicable)_____

DATE OF ANNUAL SPRING PERFORMANCE APPRAISAL_____

_____

The performance appraisal process is intended to provide a forum for the supervisor and the employee to discuss strengths, areas of improvement, and to set up goals for the coming year.

INSTRUCTIONS

Page one is to be completed by the employee and page two and three by the supervisor. When the performance appraisal process is completed, the Summary of Supervisor/Employee Performance Appraisal will become part of the employees's file.

SIMMONS COLLEGE

SUPERVISOR'S PERFORMANCE APPRAISAL OF:_____

(For Discussion Purposes)

1. Comment on the accomplishments of the employee this past year. (How has s/he performed and in what areas has s/he improved?)

2. What goal(s) for improvement should the employee set for the coming year?

3. What areas of skill or staff development would be helpful to the employee?

SIMMONS COLLEGE

CONFERENCE MEETING

SUMMARY OF SUPERVISOR/EMPLOYEE PERFORMANCE APPRAISAL

NAME OF EMPLOYEE_____ NAME OF SUPERVISOR_____

1. What agreement on goal(s) setting was made?

2. What are the areas of improvement/support that were discussed?

3. What skill/staff development activities have been encouraged?

4. Comment on the accomplishments of the employee both to the department and to the College; include areas in which the employee has exceeded job expectations.

Additional Comments:

Employee's Signature_____

Supervisor's Signature_____

Date_____

Return by March 30th to: Director of Human Resources, C-208

ARIZONA STATE UNIVERSITY LIBRARIES

IV. SELF-REVIEW AND GOALS STATEMENT

A. Content

The self-review and goals statement is the librarian's evaluation of work done on the previous year's goals, combined with a statement of goals to be accomplished in the coming year. The self-review is a critical appraisal of the level of success in meeting the goals, including any obstacles which may have prevented progress on or completion of the goals. It should also include any projects or activities which were not anticipated in the prior Goals Statement. This self-evaluation should provide the reviewer(s) with sufficient analysis to measure and evaluate the past year's performance. The goals statement should provide information sufficient to enable the reviewer(s) to understand and support the planned goals. It should include an approximation of the time commitment connected with each goal, or some other indication of its relative importance. The goals statement should also note areas where special support may be needed, e.g. administrative or staff support, equipment, financial resources.

B. Format

The format follows the three main areas of the Criteria, i.e. Job Performance, Professional Development and Contribution, and Service. Under each area the librarian lists the goals set for the previous year and describes how these goals were met. Obstacles which prevented the completion of goals should also be discussed. The narrative can be included under each goal or written after all goals are listed for that area. The second section of the document consists of a statement of goals for the next year using the librarian's current job description in the job performance area. The following is a sample format for the Self-Review and Goals Statement.

FORMAT FOR SELF-REVIEW AND GOALS STATEMENT

Name/Title
Review period
Date

SELF-REVIEW

I.   Job Performance
     (Use the main areas of your job description here)
     A.   Reference
          Goals for 1987
          1.   _____
          2.   _____
          3.   _____
          Activities
               (Narrative)

     B.   Collection Development
          Goals for 1987
          1.   _____
          2.   _____
          3.   _____
          Activities
               (Narrative)

     C.   Cataloging
          Goals for 1987
          1.   _____
          2.   _____
          3.   _____
          Activities
               (Narrative)

NOTE: The examples in the three major criteria were taken from Section D, Librarians' Handbook. Refer to that section for more complete guidelines

II. Professional Development and Contribution
          Goals for 1987
          1.   _____
          2.   _____
          3.   _____
     (Include narrative under each point as appropriate)

     A.   Continued and/or continuing education
     B.   Conferences, workshops, etc. (include date, place, subject and particular significance)
     C.   Research and publication
     D.   Professional organization activity
     E.   Teaching
     F.   Other

III. Service
          Goals for 1987
          1.   _____
          2.   _____
          3.   _____
     (Include narrative under each point as appropriate)

A. Professional memberships
B. Participation in library committees and/or u
   committees (list committees with comr
   appropriate)
C. Community activities
D. Mentoring
E. Consulting
F. Other

GOALS STATEMENT

I. <u>Job Performance</u>
(Use the main areas of your job description here)

A. Reference
Goals for 1988
1. _____
2. _____
3. _____

B. Collection Development
Goals for 1988
1. _____
2. _____
3. _____

C. Cataloging
Goals for 1988
1. _____
2. _____
3. _____

II. <u>Professional Development and Contribution</u>

Goals for 1988
1. _____
2. _____
3. _____

III. <u>Service</u>

Goals for 1988
1. _____
2. _____
3. _____

Signature_____   Date_____

Appendix A:1

LIBRARIAN SELF REVIEW AND GOAL STATEMENT

1. Using the goal statement from your last review and the
    <u>Criteria</u>, analyze and evaluate your performance and the
    accomplishment of your stated goals for the past year. This
    self-evaluation should be a critical appraisal of your
    success in meeting your goals and any obstacles that kept
    you from meeting them. Your self-evaluation should include
    all of the areas in the goal statement and provide the
    reviewer(s) with sufficient analysis to measure and evaluate
    your performance. You should include any projects or
    activities that you did not anticipate in your last goal
    statement.

2. Using the <u>Criteria</u> and the Guidelines for Interpretation,
    describe your goals and activities for the coming year. You
    should include an approximation of the time commitment
    involved with each activity so that your evaluator(s) will
    know the relative weight you believe is appropriate for each
    activity. The goal statement should be a detailed plan
    including committees, professional activities, and anything
    else relevant to the <u>Criteria</u>. You should provide
    sufficient information to help your reviewer(s) understand
    and support your plan. You should also note those areas in
    which you need additional administrative support, equipment,
    financial resources or staff support.

Signature_____Date_____

ARIZONA STATE UNIVERSITY LIBRARIES

III. GOAL SETTING

A. Introduction

ASU Libraries emphasizes strategic planning and goal setting which are designed to fulfill the mission statement of the system and improve organizational and individual performance. Each department, and ideally, each unit within a department, also develops goals and objectives to support and fulfill its portion of the Libraries' mission statement. Therefore, the formulation of individual goals is not only an exercise to facilitate writing the self-review, but is also evidence of the individual's contribution to the achievements of the ASU Libraries. Individual goals provide the framework for performance; activities in meeting those goals provide the basis for performance evaluation. Because of the fluid nature of position responsibilities it is probable that emphases within a position will fluctuate and goals will change from year to year.

B. Formulating Goals

Since individual goals are dependent upon organizational goals, it is assumed that the librarian, through the primary evaluator, will be knowledgeable concerning library and departmental goals. The librarian is responsible for formulating goals within the context of departmental and organizational goals. Goals and objectives will be written by the librarian and may reflect advisement by appropriate supplementary reviewers following the procedures in Section E.III.B. The primary evaluator will provide final judgment and guidance on the entire goals and objectives document.

1. Relation to the Job Description

The initial step in setting goals is to analyze both the librarian's current job description and past activities to identify basic responsibilities, what is actually done, and what is most important. As the job description changes (Section E.II.B), goals should also change. Goals should include the specific responsibilities listed in the job description, but will also reflect other innovative and/or creative activity.

2. Relation to Criteria

Goals should reflect the categories of the criteria for Retention, Continuing Appointment, and Promotion. The major portion will cover Job Performance goals dealing with continuing job responsibilities, i.e., maintenance goals. The statement of basic maintenance goals is critical to insure balance in the overall performance plan for the year. Other goals address specific problems or project oriented activities. Professional Development and Contribution and Service goals follow the same pattern. A goal may extend beyond one review period as a work-in-progress statement; a goal may include activities which will fall in more than one area of concentration.

3. Priorities

The librarian's goals statement should clearly reflect the priority the librarian places on each of the goals. During the review interview, the librarian and primary evaluator should reach a mutual understanding regarding the relative importance of each goal, the time commitment involved, impact on the departmental goals, and standards for accomplishment.

4. Attainability

Goals must be realistic and achievable. The librarian should identify conditions and possible obstacles to achievement. Common barriers to achieving goals include:

--individual goals set unrealistically high
--lack of balance among maintenance and high-visibility goals
--staff member diverted from area of responsibility
--changed conditions in work unit
--inadequate planning, training, and/or support
--insufficient motivation
--failure to follow established procedures
--lack of cooperation among staff or from other units

Examining the viability of goals using the above list may alert the primary evaluator and librarian to the need for restructuring goals before the review process is completed.

5. Measurability

Goals should have some measurable or observable outcome which can either be quantified or clearly described in narrative form. Examples of quantitative definition include: quantity (amount); rate (amount per time unit); time spent, or completion date. Some goals cannot be measured in quantifiable terms; a qualitative narrative measuring the outcomes by judgment and observation will record achievement.

6. Changes or Revisions

When necessary, the primary evaluator and librarian are encouraged to meet to review the librarian's progress toward achieving goals at mid-year. While not mandatory, this schedule allows recognition of unanticipated obstacles such as a change in the job description, changes in priorities, department realignments, etc. Formally negotiated amendments to the librarian's goals statement should be documented, signed and dated by the librarian, primary evaluator, and the appropriate AUL. The amended statement will become part of the formal review package.

The Libraries
Massachusetts Institute of Technology
Cambridge, Massachusetts, 02139

Office of the Director

GUIDELINES FOR THE USE OF PERFORMANCE CRITERIA AND BENCHMARKS

The attached Performance Criteria are to be used in conjunction with the annual salary review for librarians and other academic staff and for support staff. The intent of the document is to assist supervisors and department heads in arriving at an overall performance statement that can be translated centrally into a percentage increase.

The criteria are not intended to replace the judgement, often subjective judgement, of the evaluator. They are intended to serve as guidelines to the standards of performance by which all library staff are to be evaluated. Descriptors used in benchmark statements, while measurable, are not precisely quantitative and will require the evaluators exercising considerable subjective judgement in the interpretation of such terms as "effective", highly effective", "substantially exceeding", etc.

The criteria are divided into a number of factors (e.g. productivity, quality, etc.). Not all of these factors apply to each position, and those that do apply will vary in weight from position to position. The evaluator will, therefore, first need to decide which factors apply to a specific position and their relative importance.

For each factor, there are five benchmark statements numbered from 1 to 5. The first statement in each factor describes the highest level of performance related to that factor. In ascending numerical order, progressively lower levels of performance are described until unsatisfactory performance is described in the last statement. Since these are benchmark statements, they are not intended to describe all possible levels of performance. The evaluator must therefore determine which best describes overall performance related to that factor or if performance falls between two statements.

Performance must be looked at for consistency. Judgements must be made about the weight and importance of elements of performance within a factor. Since few positions in the Libraries are composed of only one function, performance within one factor area may vary from performance of one function to performance of another (e.g. in one position, performance of searching responsibilities may be carried out at Level I while performance of typing or filing may be performed at Level III).

After application of the criteria, an overall rating or evaluative statement must be made. Five levels of performance are described below. These are again benchmark statements, not intended to describe perfectly any one staff member's performance. By using pluses (+) or minuses (-), evaluators can more precisely recommend performance levels for salary reviews.

Overall Rating Benchmarks

Level I: Consistently performs all elements of the position at an exceptionally high level; services rendered or products generated are of an exceptionally high quality, are timely, and clearly reflect a thorough understanding of the principles governing the areas of responsibility and of the Libraries policies, practices and priorities. All relationships with other staff and users are exceptionally effective. Contributions to system-wide efforts have been outstanding. Is thoroughly knowledgeable in all areas pertinent to the position.

Level II: Consistently performs all major elements of the position at a level that substantially exceeds the requirements for the position; services rendered or products are of high quality, are timely, and reflect a sound understanding of the principles governing the areas of responsibility and of the Libraries policies, practices and priorities. Relationships with other staff and users are highly effective. Has made substantive contributions to system-wide efforts. Knowledge in areas related to the position is up-to-date and sound.

Level III: Consistently performs at a fully satisfactory level in meeting the requirements in all major elements of the position; services rendered or products are of a fully satisfactory quality, are timely, and reflect an understanding of the principles governing the areas of responsibility and of major Libraries policies, practices and priorities. Relationships with other staff and users are sufficiently effective to enable carrying out the responsibilities of the position satisfactorily. Contributions to system-wide efforts have usually been good. Knowledge in areas related to the position is sufficient for satisfactory performance.

Level IV: Does not consistently perform at a satisfactory level in meeting the requirements in all major elements of the position; services rendered or products are not always acceptable in quality, timeliness or quantity and do not consistently reflect an understanding of basic principles or of the Libraries policies, practices and priorities. Relationships with other staff and users are not consistently adequate to carry out the responsibilities of the position or have had a delitorious effect on other staff and users. Contributions to system-wide efforts have not consistently been satisfactory. Needs to improve knowledge in major areas related to the position in order to perform satisfactorily.

Level V: Performance has been unsatisfactory in one or more major areas of responsibility; has not successfully responded to directions and suggestions for improvement. Services rendered or products are not acceptable in terms of quality, timeliness or quantity and do not reflect an understanding of the relevant basic principles or of the Libraries policies, practices and priorities. Relationships with other staff and users are not adequate to carry out the responsibilities of the position or have a delitorious effect on other staff and users. Contributions to system-wide efforts are not satisfactory. Knowledge in major areas related to the position is insufficient to perform satisfactorily.

31 January 1985

MIT LIBRARIES PERFORMANCE EVALUATION SYSTEM
FOR LIBRARIANS AND OTHER ACADEMIC STAFF

STAFF MEMBER COPY

1. Objectives

   a. To improve the effectiveness of the MIT Libraries in achieving its goals through the continual development of individual staff members;
   b. Help staff members to grow and improve in their present job assignments, in self-development, and in setting appropriate goals for future growth.
   c. Provide staff members with an assessment of the quality of their performance.
   d. Assist in the determination of salary recommendations.
   e. Strengthen communication and understanding between staff members and their supervisors.
   f. Contribute to the identification of candidates for promotion.

2. Responsibility for Administration

   The performance review system and procedures will be administered by the Assistant Director for Administration in consultation with Steering Committee and others as appropriate. The system will be continuously reviewed, assessed, and updated.

3. Reporting Period

   a. All newly-appointed staff members, including staff members appointed to new positions, will be evaluated on the six-month anniversary of appointment.
   b. A performance evaluation of librarians and other academic staff will be conducted annually on the anniversary of the six month evaluation.

4. Participants

   a. Ordinarily, staff members will be evaluated by their immediate supervisors. In some situations, the staff member may be evaluated, at their request, by more than one supervisor, for example, the immediate supervisor and department head.

   b. Some staff members may, while administratively reporting to only one person, be responsible to different persons for different aspects of their responsibilities. It is essential in those cases that the evaluator seek input on performance from all appropriate persons before the evaluation. It is recommended that an actual evaluation of the staff member take place with each person who has a supervisory role.

   c. In a few cases it is mandated by library policy that multiple evaluations take place (e.g. collection managers are to be evaluated both by the Assistant Director for Collection Management and Technical Services and by the immediate supervisor in the divisional library.)

MIT LIBRARIES LIBRARIAN AND OTHER ACADEMIC STAFF PERFORMANCE EVALUATION
Page Two

5. Form

a. The performance evaluation may be written or oral, at the option
of the staff members being reviewed or the option of the supervisor
except as follows:
   i. Newly-appointed staff members must have written evaluations at
   the six-month anniversary of appointment.
   ii. A Librarian I must have written evaluations until promotion to
   Librarian II has occurred.
   iii. All staff members must have written evaluations at least once every three
   years unless exempted by their Assistant Director (in the case of staff
   members in the Institute Archives and in the MIT Museum, by the
   Director).

b. The forms used will be prepared by the Assistant Director for
Administration in consultation with others as appropriate; the forms
are subject to change and modification to reflect experience with
the process. The following forms are currently in use (samples are
attached):

Part I   Review of Accomplishments   (staff member)
Part II   Goal-Setting Statement   (staff member)
Part III   Performance Evaluation   (supervisor)
Part IV   Goal Setting Statement   (supervisor)
Part IV   Interview Summary Sheet   (staff member and supervisor)

6. Record Keeping

a. Written performance evaluations will be retained in the
Director's Office for three years. Supervisors will not keep copies
for their files. At the request of staff members, the written
evaluations may be made a part of their permanent personnel files.
Supervisors are encouraged to keep a copy of the summary statement
of goals agreed upon in the evaluation.

b. Access to written evaluations is limited to the individual, the
immediate supervisor and/or department heads, and Steering Committee
members.

7. Procedure

a. The forms and explanatory memoranda will be prepared by the
Assistant Director for Administration and distributed to Department
Heads by the end of the month preceding the scheduled evaluation.
Department Heads will distribute them to the staff member(s) to be
evaluated.

MIT LIBRARIES LIBRARIAN AND OTHER ACADEMIC STAFF PERFORMANCE EVALUATION
Page Three

b. The supervisor and staff member will discuss as soon as possible the nature of the evaluation (i.e. oral or written). Staff members seeking exemption from the mandatory three-year written evaluation should address a request in writing to their Assistant Director (in the case of Institute Archives and MIT Museum staff members, to the Director) stating the reason for the request.

c. Interviews will be scheduled by the supervisor; it is suggested that at least an hour for each interview be allowed.

d. Each staff member and supervisor completes forms or prepares for oral discussion. Written forms are exchanged the day before a scheduled interview.

e. Oral interview will be held during which supervisor and staff member discuss past performance and negotiate goals; goals agreed upon are to be summarized on the interview summary sheet which both supervisor and staff member then sign.

f. All forms will be forwarded by the Department Head to the Assistant Director for Administration by the end of the scheduled month for evaluation.

MIT LIBRARIES LIBRARIAN AND OTHER ACADEMIC STAFF PERFORMANCE EVALUATION

Part I
REVIEW OF ACCOMPLISHMENTS - STAFF MEMBER

This part provides an opportunity for the staff member to describe accomplishments during the past year including goals achieved, special projects, and increased responsibilities. The staff member may comment on how improvements can be made and where additional assistance or guidance might be given; also a review of the supervisor by the staff member may be included here. A second portion of the review might describe professional activities including education during the year, special assignments, active membership in professional organizations, offices held, research, and publication.

STAFF MEMBER_____

MIT LIBRARIES LIBRARIAN AND OTHER ACADEMIC STAFF PERFORMANCE EVALUATION

Part II
GOAL-SETTING STATEMENT - STAFF MEMBER

The staff member should describe goals for the coming year for regular assignments, special projects, and professional development.

STAFF MEMBER_____

MIT LIBRARIES PERFORMANCE EVALUATION SYSTEM
FOR LIBRARIANS AND OTHER ACADEMIC STAFF

1. Objectives   SUPERVISOR COPY

   a. To improve the effectiveness of the MIT Libraries in achieving its goals
       through the continual development of individual staff members;
   b. Help staff members to grow and improve in their present job assignments,
       in self-development, and in setting appropriate goals for future growth.
   c. Provide staff members with an assessment of the quality of their performance.
   d. Assist in the determination of salary recommendations.
   e. Strengthen communication and understanding between staff members and their
       supervisors.
   f. Contribute to the identification of candidates for promotion.

2. Responsibility for Administration

       The performance review system and procedures will be administered by
       the Assistant Director for Administration in consultation with
       Steering Committee and others as appropriate. The system will be
       continuously reviewed, assessed, and updated.

3. Reporting Period

   a. All newly-appointed staff members, including staff members
       appointed to new positions, will be evaluated on the six-month
       anniversary of appointment.
   b. A performance evaluation of librarians and other academic staff
       will be conducted annually on the anniversary of the six month
       evaluation.

4. Participants

   a. Ordinarily, staff members will be evaluated by their immediate
       supervisors. In some situations, the staff member may be evaluated,
       at their request, by more than one supervisor, for example, the
       immediate supervisor and department head.

   b. Some staff members may, while administratively reporting to only
       one person, be responsible to different persons for different
       aspects of their responsibilities. It is essential in those cases
       that the evaluator seek input on performance from all appropriate
       persons before the evaluation. It is recommended that an actual
       evaluation of the staff member take place with each person who has a
       supervisory role.

   c. In a few cases it is mandated by library policy that multiple
       evaluations take place (e.g. collection managers are to be evaluated
       both by the Assistant Director for Collection Management and
       Technical Services and by the immediate supervisor in the divisional
       library.)

MIT LIBRARIES LIBRARIAN AND OTHER ACADEMIC STAFF PERFORMANCE EVALUATION
Page Two

5. Form

   a. The performance evaluation may be written or oral, at the option of the staff members being reviewed or the option of the supervisor except as follows:

      i. Newly-appointed staff members must have written evaluations at the six-month anniversary of appointment.

      ii. A Librarian I must have written evaluations until promotion to Librarian II has occurred.

      iii. All staff members must have written evaluations at least once every three years unless exempted by their Assistant Director (in the case of staff members in the Institute Archives and in the MIT Museum, by the Director).

   b. The forms used will be prepared by the Assistant Director for Administration in consultation with others as appropriate; the forms are subject to change and modification to reflect experience with the process. The following forms are currently in use (samples are attached):

Part I	Review of Accomplishments	(staff member)
Part II	Goal-Setting Statement	(staff member)
Part III	Performance Evaluation	(supervisor)
Part IV	Goal Setting Statement	(supervisor)
Part IV	Interview Summary Sheet	(staff member and supervisor)

6. Record Keeping

   a. Written performance evaluations will be retained in the Director's Office for three years. Supervisors will not keep copies for their files. At the request of staff members, the written evaluations may be made a part of their permanent personnel files. Supervisors are encouraged to keep a copy of the summary statement of goals agreed upon in the evaluation.

   b. Access to written evaluations is limited to the individual, the immediate supervisor and/or department heads, and Steering Committee members.

7. Procedure

   a. The forms and explanatory memoranda will be prepared by the Assistant Director for Administration and distributed to Department Heads by the end of the month preceding the scheduled evaluation. Department Heads will distribute them to the staff member(s) to be evaluated.

MIT LIBRARIES LIBRARIAN AND OTHER ACADEMIC STAFF PERFORMANCE EVALUATION
Page Three

b. The supervisor and staff member will discuss as soon as possible
the nature of the evaluation (i.e. oral or written). Staff members
seeking exemption from the mandatory three-year written evaluation
should address a request in writing to their Assistant Director (in
the case of Institute Archives and MIT Museum staff members, to the
Director) stating the reason for the request.

c. Interviews will be scheduled by the supervisor; it is suggested that
at least an hour for each interview be allowed.

d. Each staff member and supervisor completes forms or prepares for
oral discussion. Written forms are exchanged the day before a
scheduled interview.

e. Oral interview will be held during which supervisor and staff member
discuss past performance and negotiate goals; goals agreed upon are
to be summarized on the interview summary sheet which both
supervisor and staff member then sign.

f. All forms will be forwarded by the Department Head to the Assistant
Director for Administration by the end of the scheduled month for
evaluation.

MIT LIBRARIES LIBRARIAN AND OTHER ACADEMIC STAFF PERFORMANCE EVALUATION

Name_____

Part III
PERFORMANCE EVALUATION - SUPERVISOR

This part is a review of the staff member's performance and is prepared by the supervisor concurrently with the preparation of Parts I and II. The following areas may serve as guidelines where appropriate:

1.   Initiative. Comment on ability to act decisively, effectively,and at appropriate times; to be resourceful in dealing with complex as well as routine situations; and to anticipate needs and take necessary action without being directed to do so.

2.   Judgement and decision-making. Comment on the staff member's ability to consider the long-term, and system-wide consequences of decisions made; and to apply good judgement in work situations.

3.   Professional development. Consider activities over and above the regular job assignment that have had a bearing on professional growth.

4.   Professional knowledge. Consider ability to apply professional knowledge effectively in order to implement job responsibilities and the policies of the department or the MIT Libraries.

5.   Quality of work. Consider the degree of excellence of a completed assignment in view of the amount of time and effort expended; also consider thoroughness in following to completion.

6.   Quantity of work. Comment on ability to plan, organize, and schedule work, to set and meet realistic performance goals; to carry work load involving varied and concurrent activities; and to handle special assignments.

7.   Relations with other people; communications. Comment on ability to build and maintain good relations with colleagues, users and others; to cooperate with members of own and other departments; to respond positively to criticism; and to communicate effectively with supervisor.

8.   Supervisory skills (if appropriate). Comment on ability to select, place, and train personnel; to assist and to delegate work; to define authority and responsibility; to guide and lead; to produce an effective working team; to conduct objective performance appraisals, and to promote and encourage staff development.

MIT LIBRARIES LIBRARIAN AND OTHER ACADEMIC STAFF PERFORMANCE EVALUATION

Name_____

Part III (cont'd)

SUPERVISOR_____

MIT LIBRARIES LIBRARIAN AND OTHER ACADEMIC STAFF PERFORMANCE EVALUATION

Name_____

Part IV
GOAL SETTING STATEMENT - SUPERVISOR

In this section the supervisor should describe briefly major goals the staff
member should attempt to achieve during the next evaluation period. These
should form the basis for discussion of expectations the supervisor has for
the staff member as well as needs the staff member may have for support in
order to achieve them, as well as how the results may be evaluated.

SUPERVISOR_____

MIT LIBRARIES ACADEMIC STAFF PERFORMANCE EVALUATION

Part V
INTERVIEW SUMMARY SHEET

To be used to indicate any changes or goals agreed upon. Please also
indicate whether these forms are to be retained in the staff member's
permanent personnel file.

[Signed]

STAFF MEMBER_____   SUPERVISOR_____

PERFORMANCE CRITERIA AND BENCHMARKS FOR MIT LIBRARIES STAFF MEMBERS

Productivity:

Quantity of work produced.
Adherence to schedules and timeliness.
Adherence to priorities.
Ability to organize a variety of responsibilities and duties.

1. Is exceptionally productive; substantially exceeeds requirements for the position for productivity on a consistent basis; organizes own work very effectively for accomplishment; meets all deadlines and schedules with little or no direction; accomplishes all high priority assignments; manages time very effectively.

2. Is very productive; consistently exceeds requirements for the position for productivity; meets deadlines and schedules for all important projects; adheres to priorities; organizes own work effectively and makes good use of time.

3. Meets requirements of the position for productivity at a fully satisfactory level; usually meets deadlines and schedules, but may need some direction; follows priority guidelines; usually makes good use of time; occasionally needs some help in organizing work for accomplishment.

4. Does not consistently meet requirements of the position for productivity; misses deadlines and falls behind schedule and/or needs to be reminded too frequently; needs too much assistance in organizing work; needs too much direction in establishing priorities and maintaining workflow.

5. Fails to meet on a consistent basis the minimum productivity requirements for the position; has not satisfactorily responded to directions and suggestions for improvement.

Quality of Work Accomplished:

Accuracy and thoroughness.
Technical knowledge and expertise.
Understanding of objectives and goals.
Problem solving ability.
Judgement in the application of available methods.

1. Work is consistently of the highest quality; rarely, if ever, makes mistakes; thoroughly understands principles, policies and procedures governing area of assignment; provides sound solutions to complex problems independently.

2. Quality of work exceeds requirements of the position; makes few errors; has good understanding of principles, policies and procedures applicable to area of responsibility; solves routine problems independently and has good ideas for solutions to more complex problems.

3. Quality of work consistently meets requirements for the position; makes average number of errors but reflects understanding of the basic principles, policies and procedures pertinent to responsibilities; solves most routines problems satisfactorily; often needs assistance on more complex problems.

4. Makes above average number of mistakes; cannot consistently be relied on to apply principles, policies and procedures governing areas of responsibility; relies too heavily on others for solutions to routine problems; often does not recognize problem situations.

5. Quality of work is unsatisfactory; quality of work does not reflect a sufficient understanding of basic principles related to areas of responsibility; frequently does not follow applicable policies and procedures; has not satisfactorily responded to directions and guidance provided to improve quality level.

Participation in System-Wide Efforts.

Participation in meetings and discussions.
Leadership in groups and committees.
Representation of constituency.
Recognition of system-wide priorities.

1. Highly effective contributor to system-wide efforts; can be depended on to make substantive contributions; completes assignments on time and comes prepared for agenda items distributed in advance; is highly effective leader in group efforts but can follow others' leadership when appropriate; understands the system's philosophy and knows when to apply it; communicates effectively with constituency and synthesizes their issues and concerns to others clearly and objectively.

2. Makes valuable contributions to system-wide efforts; participates enthusiastically in group discussions and meetings; can go beyond own role to see broader system-wide needs and priorities; completes assignments on time and comes to meetings prepared; leads group efforts and discussions well; serves effectively as representative of constituency.

3. Contributes satisfactorily to system-wide efforts and group discussions; usually reflects understanding of system's philosophy and can rise above parochial interests; is usually prepared for meetings and discussions and can usually be depended on to complete assignments on time; needs to improve skills in leading group efforts and discussions; represents constituency satisfactorily.

4. Often has negative impact on group discussions and in meetings; contributes little or dominates discussions; often reflects parochial interests rather than system's philosophy; is often not prepared for

discussions or has not completed assignments; needs to improve both leadership abilities and ability to participate in group efforts.

5. Does not perform satisfactorily in groups and does not contribute satisfactorily in group discussions and meetings; frequently is not prepared or has not completed assignments; demonstrates little or no understanding of system's philosophy; has not responded to directions and guidance provided for improvements.

Responsibility.

Commitment to MIT and the Libraries.
Dependability.
Response to pressure or crises.

1. Is thoroughly committed to MIT and the Libraries; can always be depended on when there is a need to get something done; makes extra effort to get urgent things done; responds effectively under pressure or when there is a crisis.

2. Commitment to MIT and the Libraries is commendable; often makes extra effort to get the job done; is very dependable; works well under pressure.

3. Is usually reliable; commitment to position is satisfactory; occasionally makes extra effort when there is a high priority need; work is satisfactory when under pressure.

4. Displays little commitment to position; rarely makes extra effort even when there is an urgent need; does not work well under pressure.

5. Has not been dependable; does not make even minimal effort to get the job done even when there are high priority needs; work is unsatisfactory under pressure; has not responded satisfactorily to directions and suggestions for improvement.

Interpersonal Skills.

Relationships with users, supervisees, supervisors, peers and others relevant to the responsibilities of the position.
Communication skills (oral and written).
Participation in discussions and meetings.
Contributions to group efforts.

1. Maintains extremely effective working relationships with others; communicates with all pertinent groups with high degree of effectiveness; makes outstanding contributions to group efforts and discussions.

2. Maintains good working relationships with appropriate groups and persons which positively affect performance; communicates well; works well in group situations and has a positive impact on group dynamics.

3. Working relationships are satisfactory and are rarely inhibiting factors on own performance or the performance of others; communications are usually satisfactory; usually contributes satisfactorily to group efforts.

4. Needs to improve working relationships so that they do not inhibit own performance or the performance of others; needs to communicate with others more clearly and effectively; often has negative impact on group efforts and discussions.

5. Has been unable to develop and maintain satisfactory working relationships; does not communicate with others effectively; has not consistently performed satisfactorily in group efforts; has not responded to assistance given for improvement.

Self-Development.

Awareness of developments in area of expertise.
Contributions to profession.
Service to MIT community outside areas of responsibility, particularly those which would stimulate self-development.

1. Is extremely active in developmental pursuits which have led to substantial growth in knowledge and skills pertinent to areas of responsibility; has made substantive contributions to the profession or the MIT community; is constantly looking for ways to improve skills and abilities; applies new knowledge and skills to the Libraries' programs and activities effectively.

2. Keeps up-to-date on developments pertinent to area of expertise; knows current issues and their applicability to areas of responsibility; makes appropriate contributions to the profession or the MIT community; takes responsibility for own development and applies new knowledge and skills appropriately in carrying out responsibilities.

3. Follows up on suggestions for developmental activities which could improve skills and knowledge; maintains satisfactory awareness of issues and developments related to area of responsibility.

4. Knowledge and understanding of new developments in area of expertise is not sufficient; needs to be more active in self-development and needs to improve skills and knowledge in areas related to own responsibilities.

5. Has not been active in developmental pursuits which has had a negative impact on performance; is not sufficiently aware of new developments and issues pertinent to own areas of responsibility; has not responded to suggestions for improvement.

Other Pertinent Factors.

Initiative.
Adaptability.
Objectivity.
Stability.
Responsiveness to instruction/criticism.

1. Takes initative for innovation; adapts well to changes in the organization and in matters related to area of responsibility; can be relied on for objectivity and stability when conflicts arise; seeks consensus; readily accepts instruction and criticism and looks for ways to learn or improve.

2. Readily accepts new ideas and often takes the initiative for change; maintains open-minded, calm approach to controversy; is a positive influence in achieving consensus; reacts positively to criticism and instruction and adjusts behavior or performance accordingly.

3. Is usually receptive to new ideas; adapts to changes satisfactorily; is usually objective and listens to all sides in controversies; accepts instruction and criticism appropriately.

4. Has difficulty adapting to change and may occasionally resist new ideas and innovations; cannot be relied on for objectivity when conflicts or controversies arise; does not accept instruction or criticism well.

5. Resists change and new ideas; is often opinionated or easily prejudiced when conflicts or controversies arise; does not respond to instruction or criticism well; has not satisfactorily responded to directions and suggestions for improvements in this area.

Supervisory Elements.

Fairness and judgement in personnel decisions.
Training and orientation.
Performance evaluation.
Accessibility to staff.
Delegation of responsibility.
Encouragement of staff development.
Motivation of staff.
Communication with staff.
Ability to set priorities for staff.

1. Consistently exercises exceptional judgement in personnel decisions, reflecting a sound understanding of personnel policies; defines jobs for effectively carrying out responsibilities and sets realistic performance goals; consistently hires high quality staff members with appropriate skills and abilities and provides effective training and orientation programs; is consistent, fair and objective in recommendations for promotion, in performance evaluations and in dealing with performance problems; gives timely and appropriate feedback to staff members on performance on a regular basis;

sets priorities for staff that ensure accomplishment of all of the highest priorities; encourages staff to develop skills and abilities further and to apply them; maintains appropriate level of accessibility to staff to answer questions and solve problems; understands workflow and its impacts on other library operations and activities; makes excellent use of delegation and motivates staff to high levels of accomplishment; communicates well with staff and keeps them informed on all appropriate matters related to their work; encourages good communication among staff members.

2. Consistently makes sound personnel decisions, reflecting a good understanding of personnel policies; defines jobs well and clearly defines tasks to be done; hires appropriate staff members and provides good training and orientation programs; is fair and objective in recommendations for promotions, in performance evaluations and in dealing with performance problems; sets reasonable performance goals and provides feedback on accomplishments or deficiencies; encourages staff development and suggests training opportunities; is usually available to the staff for questions and problems; delegates appropriate responsibilities and authority and motivates staff well; maintains good communications with staff and keeps them abreast of most relevant information.

3. Usually can be relied on to make satisfactory personnel decisions but requires some assistance and advice on a regular basis; usually hires good staff members and provides relevant training and orientation; is usually fair and objective in recommendations for promotions, in performance evaluations and in dealing with performance problems; needs some assistance in setting reasonable performance goals; usually provides appropriate feedback to staff members on accomplishments; maintains adequate accessibility to staff members for questions and problems and usually can satisfy their needs; is aware of the impact of workflow on other library activities and operations but often needs some assistance in identifying them completely; motivates staff adequately; staff is usually aware of relevant information that affects their areas of responsibility.

4. Needs to improve supervisory techniques; requires too much direction in arriving at good personnel decisions and in developing jobs and defining tasks; cannot be relied on to identify appropriate skills and abilities in hiring new staff members; needs to improve training and orientation programs; has not consistently maintained objectivity in recommending personnel actions, in performance evaluations and in dealing with performance problems; does not motivate staff members well; too frequently is not available to staff members or cannot answer their questions or solve their more complex problems; needs to improve communications with and among staff members.

5. Supervisory responsibilities have not been carried out satisfactorily and has not successfully made improvements in this area; does not make good personnel decisions with any consistency and seems not to understand personnel management principles; does not make good hiring decisions; does not provide adequate training and orientation; frequently lacks objectivity in recommendations for personnel actions, in performance evaluations and in dealing with performance problems; is not able consistently to answer staff members' questions or to solve their problems; has difficulty understanding workflow and its impact on other library activities; communications with and among staff members has not been satisfactory.

Managerial Elements.

Planning.
Organizing and administering.
Setting priorities, objectives and goals.
Financial management
Adherence to system-wide policies and procedures.
Support of system-wide obejctives and priorities.
Leadership.
Creating high morale environment.

1. Is a highly effective manager; sets highly effective objectives and goals and organizes functions effectively to carry out the unit's responsibilities; is responsive to needs and sets priorities effectively to meet them within available resources; administers unit with exceptional effectiveness; identifies options, weighs costs and benefits carefully and can be relied on to make sound management decisions; takes calculated risks but can be depended on not to make rash decisions; makes highly effective use of available resources; stays within budget and ensures that funds available for unit's activities are spent wisely; supports system-wide philosophy and policies and adheres to them carefully; creates an environment that stimulates and challenges staff members to high levels of achievement and consistently provides effective leadership.

2. Is a good manager; sets objectives and goals that are appropriate and responsive to needs; sets appropriate priorities for the unit; uses available resources well; provides effective administration; makes good management decisions based on available information; cautious in taking risks and may need some encouragement but follows a good process for identifying and weighing options; good financial manager; stays within budget; adheres to Institute and Libraries policies and supports system-wide goals; provides good leadership and stimulates good morale within unit.

3. Manages unit satisfactorily; usually sets objectives and goals that are appropriate to needs; priorities established for unit are usually appropriate not creative in using available resources; management decisions usually reflect a satisfactory process of decision making; usually stays within budget or within a reasonable percentage of overage; usually follows established policies and practices; provides adequate level of leadership; morale of staff is not usually a problem.

4. Needs to improve management practice; needs too much assistance in establishing appropriate objectives and goals for unit and in setting priorities; cannot be relied on to have reached management decisions carefully; financial management needs improvement; overspends or underspends budget consistently and by an unsatisfactory margin; does not provide adequate leadership to unit; morale of staff needs to be improved.

5. Management practices are consistently unsatisfactory and has not responded satisfactorily to direction and guidance given to improve performance as a manager; is inconsistent in setting appropriate objectives and goals and in setting priorities that respond to needs; does not think issues through to

arrive at meaningful decisions; poor financial management has led to serious budgetary problems and to poor use of resources; leadership for unit has been inadequate and has had serious impact on morale of unit.

31 January 1985

Aurora Public Schools
1085 Peoria Street
Aurora, Colorado 80011

GENERAL GUIDELINES
FOR THE EVALUATION
OF TEACHERS IN
THE AURORA PUBLIC SCHOOLS

Section IV

Procedures for the
Evaluation of:

Media Specialists

EFFECTIVE
SEPTEMBER 1986

Prepared by
The Committee to Review
and Revise the Guidelines
for the Evaluation of Teachers

Personnel Services Division

PERFORMANCE EVALUATION-MEDIA SPECIALIST

1. This form is to be used to evaluate media specialists in the elementary, middle, senior high and vocational schools.

2. In addition to observations, relevant sources of documentation of performance are attached and/or cited in the evaluation.

3. An "X" placed in an unacceptable box will require a written comment by the evaluator. Comments are encouraged for "X's" placed in other boxes.

4. Refer to the Performance Descriptor list for items that may have been used as references for the evaluation.

EXPLANATION OF PERFORMANCE STANDARDS

The categories provided on the Performance Evaluation Form for evaluation of the staff member's performance, should be interpreted to convey the following meanings:

Superior   The highest evaluation which can be earned. This is demonstrated by the highest quality of competence which is possessed by relatively few staff members.

Very Good   Performance that is typical of thoroughly satisfactory and competent performance. It is anticipated that many staff members will receive this evaluation.

Acceptable   Performance is satisfactory and creditable. Generally consistent with performance observed in the average or slightly above average situation.

Unacceptable   Performance which appears to be generally substandard. An Unacceptable rating in any category may be cause for termination or nonrenewal of contract.

ⓐ Aurora Public Schools
1085 Peoria Street
Aurora Colorado 80011

PERFORMANCE EVALUATION-MEDIA SPECIALIST
(See Reverse Side for More Detail)

Staff Member Initial _____
Evaluator Initial _____

NAME _____ DATE _____

ASSIGNMENT _____

LOCATION _____

YRS 1st _____ 3rd _____
APS 2nd _____ Tenure _____

This evaluation is based in part on the following formal observations:

Date Held	Observed by
_____	_____
_____	_____
_____	_____

PERFORMANCE STANDARDS

1. Human Relations: Establishes good rapport with a) students, b) parents, and c) colleagues. _____

	Unacceptable	Acceptable	Very Good	Superior
a.	☐	☐	☐	☐
b.	☐	☐	☐	☐
c.	☐	☐	☐	☐

2. Media Area Competencies: a) Participates in curricula implementation, b) keeps abreast of developments in the field, c) evidences utilization of appropriate resources. _____

	Unacceptable	Acceptable	Very Good	Superior
a.	☐	☐	☐	☐
b.	☐	☐	☐	☐
c.	☐	☐	☐	☐

3. Instructional Techniques: Exhibits the use of effective and diversified methods to impact instruction. _____

	Unacceptable	Acceptable	Very Good	Superior
a.	☐	☐	☐	☐

4. Media Center Management: a) Plans, organizes and executes the media program, b) enhances the efforts of students and staff. _____

	Unacceptable	Acceptable	Very Good	Superior
a.	☐	☐	☐	☐
b.	☐	☐	☐	☐

5. Other Professional Aspects of Staff Member Performance: If used, please specify. _____

	Unacceptable	Acceptable	Very Good	Superior
a.	☐	☐	☐	☐

District Form 1040 (7-86)

page 1 of 2

PERFORMANCE EVALUATION

Name_____

Summary of Strengths/Weaknesses

Recommendations/Suggestions for Improvement

Reviewed with Individual Evaluated on_____ _____ _____

Date   Signature of Evaluator   Position

Comments of Individual Evaluated (Optional)

_____ _____

Date   Signature of Individual Being Evaluated

The signature on this form of the individual being evaluated does not necessarily indicate agreement of disagreement with the contents of the evaluation, but does indicate that the individual has reviewed the evaluation with the evaluator. If the individual being evaluated wishes to submit a separate statement, it must be signed and submitted to the evaluator in duplicate within fifteen working days of the date the evaluation is signed by the evaluator.

Reviewed By _____ _____ Distribute as Follows
(Permanent File   Instructional   Personnel   1. Permanent File (white)
copy only)   Services   Services   2. Person Evaluated (yellow)
                        3. Evaluator (pink)

District Form 1041 (7-86)   page 2 of 2

PERFORMANCE DESCRIPTOR LIST - MEDIA SPECIALIST

1. Descriptors - Human Relations

   a. Students
      1) Exhibits respect for students.
      2) Is respected by students.
      3) Expresses genuine empathy and concern for all students.
      4) Is fair, impartial and objective in treatment of students.
      5) Is available to students; offers additional assistance.
      6) Uses constructive criticism and is supportive of the students.
      7) Allows students' constructive suggestions.
      8) Respects the integrity and individual differences of students.
      9) Interacts well with students.
      10) Brings student concerns to attention of appropriate personnel.

   b. Parents
      1) Communicates with parents regarding student's progress.
      2) Exhibits respect for parents.
      3) Is respected by parents.
      4) Addresses parental concerns immediately.
      5) Does mutual planning with parents, when necessary.
      6) Maintains a professional decorum when dealing with parents.

   c. Colleagues
      1) Uses discretion and respect in speaking of colleagues.
      2) Exhibits respect for other staff.
      3) Is respected by other staff.
      4) Cooperates with administrators and keeps them informed.
      5) Accepts constructive criticism and guidance.
      6) Utilizes and works courteously and cooperatively with teaching staff, para-professionals and other support personnel.
      7) Utilizes appropriate organizational channels in dealing with problems/issues.

2. Descriptors - Media Area Competencies

   a. Curriculum participation
      1) Participates with staff in curricular planning, development and revision.
      2) Works cooperatively with staff in utilization of appropriate media and instructional strategies.
      3) Provides media services, guidance and resources appropriate to the users' needs, interests and abilities.
      4) Participates, as assigned, with District curriculum committees.

   b. Keeps abreast of developments in the field
      1) Displays a constructive attitude toward professional growth.
      2) Continues to improve competence by taking applicable professional advancement courses, institutes, and workshops.

   c. Utilization of appropriate resources
      1) Coordinates procedures for selection, processing and cataloging media materials and equipment according to District guidelines.

2) Provides for arranging and circulating media materials and equipment for effective utilization in the instructional program.

3) Maintains the building collection of materials and equipment in good condition through inventory, weeding and repairing.

4) Develops a plan for collection development utilizing recognized tools such as collection mapping.

5) Uses available and appropriate technology in the management of resources.

6) Coordinates media technology and available production facilities and services to support the instructional program.

7) Provides integration of equipment into the instructional process.

8) Coordinates the retrieval of materials and information through a variety of community resources including inter-library loan and networking as needed.

9) Facilitates the preparation of bibliographies in response to requests by students and staff.

3. Descriptors - Instructional Techniques

a. To provide a positive learning environment
1) Exercises a leadership role in encouraging media utilization by students and staff.
2) Orients students and staff to the library media center and its services.
3) Participates in the facilitation of student learning activities which may be done in the classroom as well as in the media center.
4) Coordinates and participates in the implementation of the Aurora Public Schools Media Skills Guideline program.
5) Assists students in selection of materials and equipment.
6) Provides formal and/or informal inservice training as needed; e.g., equipment, materials and new technologies.
7) Provides guidance in the development of discriminating reading, viewing and listening habits.
8) Provides assistance and instruction as appropriate to students and teachers for production of learning materials.

4. Descriptors - Media Center Management

a. To plan, organize and execute those responsibilities pertaining to the media program.
1) Develops a plan, priorities and evaluation for the media program in consultation with the principal and staff.
2) Assesses needs and available resources and designs and manages the annual budget based on District and building goals.
3) Coordinates the acquisition, organization, distribution and retrieval of media resources and equipment using approved policies.
4) Assists the principal, as directed, in assessment of the media center staff.
5) Compiles and maintains informational records and reports as necessary.
6) Designs and participates in the routine operations of the media center as necessary; e.g., circulation, equipment repair, shelving materials, etc.

b.   To enhance, strengthen and support the efforts and interests of students and staff.

     1) Manages library media facilities for flexibility, accessibility and attractiveness.

     2) Publicizes and promotes the services and resources available to students and staff.

     3) Coordinates special library related activities; e.g., book fairs, book exchanges, book distribution programs, displays, read-a-thons, and the like.

     4) Participates with the principal in developing a system to provide regular communication about media services with staff, students and volunteers.

5.   <u>Descriptors - Other Professional Aspects of Performance</u>

a.

     1) Abides by staff decisions.

     2) Adheres to and enforces School Board policies and procedures and established building procedures.

     3) Is not absent from the classroom unnecessarily.

     4) Is prompt in meeting responsibilities.

     5) Is physically and emotionally able to perform assigned duties.

     6) Meets the workday time requirement.

     7) Is flexible and able to cope with adversity.

     8) Displays an enthusiasm for teaching.

     9) Is neat and clean in appearance.

ARIZONA STATE UNIVERSITY LIBRARIES

PERFORMANCE ANALYSIS FOR CLASSIFIED PERSONNEL

NAME: _____   POSITION: _____

DEPARTMENT/   ANNIVERSARY   EVALUATION
DIVISION: _____   DATE: _____   DATE: _____

TYPE OF EVALUATION: ANNUAL ____   PROBATIONARY: 2 MONTH ____   5 MONTH ____

REVIEW OF JOB DESCRIPTION: NO CHANGE NECESSARY _____   UPDATE ATTACHED ____

FOR EACH APPLICABLE CATEGORY, PLEASE CIRCLE APPROPRIATE SCORE
AND ADD EXPLANATORY COMMENTS.

KNOWLEDGE			COMMENTS
Outstanding	4		
Very Good	3.5	3	
Satisfactory	2.5	2	
Marginal	1.5	1	
Unsatisfactory	0		

JUDGMENT			COMMENTS
Outstanding	4		
Very Good	3.5	3	
Satisfactory	2.5	2	
Marginal	1.5	1	
Unsatisfactory	0		

QUALITY OF WORK			COMMENTS
Outstanding	4		
Very Good	3.5	3	
Satisfactory	2.5	2	
Marginal	1.5	1	
Unsatisfactory	0		

4/7/88

EFFICIENCY   COMMENTS

Outstanding	4	
Very Good	3.5	3
Satisfactory	2.5	2
Marginal	1.5	1
Unsatisfactory	0	

RELATIONS WITHIN THE
DEPARTMENT: CO-WORKERS   COMMENTS

Outstanding	4	
Very Good	3.5	3
Satisfactory	2.5	2
Marginal	1.5	1
Unsatisfactory	0	

RELATIONS WITHIN THE
DEPARTMENT: SUBORDINATES   COMMENTS

Outstanding	4	
Very Good	3.5	3
Satisfactory	2.5	2
Marginal	1.5	1
Unsatisfactory	0	

RELATIONS WITHIN THE
DEPARTMENT: SUPERVISOR   COMMENTS

Outstanding	4	
Very Good	3.5	3
Satisfactory	2.5	2
Marginal	1.5	1
Unsatisfactory	0	

RELATIONS WITH PERSONNEL FROM OTHER
DEPARTMENTS AND/OR THE GENERAL PUBLIC   COMMENTS

Outstanding	4	
Very Good	3.5	3
Satisfactory	2.5	2
Marginal	1.5	1
Unsatisfactory	0	

INITIATIVE   COMMENTS

Outstanding	4	
Very Good	3.5	3
Satisfactory	2.5	2
Marginal	1.5	1
Unsatisfactory	0	

ADAPTABILITY   COMMENTS

Outstanding	4	
Very Good	3.5	3
Satisfactory	2.5	2
Marginal	1.5	1
Unsatisfactory	0	

MANAGEMENT SKILLS:
MANAGING WORKFLOW OF OTHERS   COMMENTS

Outstanding	4	
Very Good	3.5	3
Satisfactory	2.5	2
Marginal	1.5	1
Unsatisfactory	0	
Not Applicable	_____	

MANAGEMENT SKILLS:
SELECTING AND EVALUATING SUBORDINATES   COMMENTS

Outstanding	4	
Very Good	3.5	3
Satisfactory	2.5	2
Marginal	1.5	1
Unsatisfactory	0	
Not Applicable	_____	

MANAGEMENT SKILLS:
TRAINING ABILITY   COMMENTS

Outstanding	4	
Very Good	3.5	3
Satisfactory	2.5	2
Marginal	1.5	1
Unsatisfactory	0	
Not Applicable	_____	

MANAGEMENT SKILLS: MAKING DECISIONS
SOLVING PROBLEMS, PROVIDING LEADERSHIP   COMMENTS

Outstanding	4	
Very Good	3.5	3
Satisfactory	2.5	2
Marginal	1.5	1
Unsatisfactory	0	
Not Applicable	_____	

DEPENDABILITY   COMMENTS

Outstanding	4	
Very Good	3.5	3
Satisfactory	2.5	2
Marginal	1.5	1
Unsatisfactory	0	

<u>ATTENDANCE</u>   <u>COMMENTS</u>

Outstanding   4

Very Good   3.5   3

Satisfactory   2.5   2

Marginal   1.5   1

Unsatisfactory   0

<u>CONTRIBUTIONS TO THE MISSION OF THE</u>
<u>DEPARTMENT AND THE LIBRARIES IN GENERAL</u>   <u>COMMENTS</u>

Outstanding   4

Very Good   3.5   3

Not Applicable   _____

Please note that, if this section is rated, it is given a value of 0.75, not 1.0, in order not to skew the ratings. That is, if all 17 sections are rated, the divisor to be used below is 16.75, not 17.00.

_____   _____   _____   _____
 TOTAL POINTS   DIVIDED BY   # SECTIONS RATED   =   AVERAGE SCORE

<u>ADDITIONAL COMMENTS BY SUPERVISOR, IDENTIFYING STRENGTHS AND WEAKNESSES & MAK-</u>
<u>ING SPECIFIC SUGGESTIONS TO IMPROVE PERFORMANCE.   USE ADD'L PAGE IF NECESSARY.</u>

RATER'S SIGNATURE _____ DATE _____

DEPT. HEAD'S SIGNATURE _____ DATE _____

AUL'S INITIALS _____

<u>TO THE EMPLOYEE BEING EVALUATED</u>:

To assist you in your effort to do a good job, conclusions based upon the manner in which you have been doing your job are summarized in this report, which will be filed with the Library Administration and the University Personnel Department.

If you would like to comment on your job performance or on any aspect of this evaluation, please do so in the space provided below. (Your comments are encouraged but not required.)

If you seriously disagree with the content of this evaluation and would prefer not to comment on the form itself, you may obtain a "Request for Review" form from the Hayden Library Administration Office.

<u>EMPLOYEE COMMENTS</u>

I have read and discussed this report with my supervisor.   I would like to have a copy of the report: Yes _____   No _____

EMPLOYEE'S SIGNATURE _____ DATE _____

ARIZONA STATE UNIVERSITY LIBRARIES
GUIDELINES FOR PERFORMANCE ANALYSIS OF CLASSIFIED STAFF

KNOWLEDGE

Consider extent to which the employee understands all phases of operation and methods required for the position.

Outstanding: Thoroughly understands all phases of job; demonstrates broad general knowledge of function & goals of dept. & library.

Very Good: Understands all phases of job; makes inquiries & asks questions when unusual circumstances are encountered.

Satisfactory: Has basic knowledge of job procedures; occasionally needs follow-up on job activity.

Marginal: Has some knowledge of job duties & procedures; regularly requires instruction & assistance.

Unsatisfactory: Lacks knowledge of job; needs close supervision; shows little evidence of improvement.

JUDGMENT

Consider how job knowledge is used in analyzing situations & making decisions. Consider also the employee's ability to recognize the limitations of his/her knowledge (e.g., to know when & whom to ask for further assistance).

Outstanding: Handles unusual or difficult situations well; understands the ramifications of various alternatives & makes consistently reliable decisions; is aware of own limitations & questions correct sources; requires very little supervision.

Very Good: Consistently makes reliable decisions, with few errors in judgment; recognizes own limitations; knows when to ask for help & asks pertinent questions; requires little supervision.

Satisfactory: Recognizes & solves frequently encountered problems; is aware of own limitations & asks questions or seeks assistance; usually makes reliable decisions with few errors in judgment; requires normal amount of supervision.

Marginal: Is inconsistent in recognizing &/or solving problems; needs to ask more questions of supervisor; does not recognize own limitations; makes frequent errors in judgment; needs close supervision.

Unsatisfactory: Displays inability to recognize &/or solve problems; does not consider consequences of decisions made; rarely asks questions or asks inappropriate questions; needs an inordinate amount of direct supervision.

4/7/88

QUALITY OF WORK

Consider the thoroughness and accuracy with which the employee's work meets and exceeds job requirements.

Outstanding: Produces work that is consistently complete, correct & legible; considers departmental goals in devising effective methods of avoiding errors &/or correcting errors; rarely makes errors in finished work.

Very Good: Produces work that is almost always complete, correct & legible; devises & uses effective methods to check work, resulting in very few errors in finished work.

Satisfactory: Produces work that is usually complete, correct & legible; checks own work; detects & corrects most errors.

Marginal: Produces work that is sometimes incomplete, incorrect or illegible; rarely uses methods for checking work, or uses methods that are ineffective, resulting in unacceptable errors in finished work.

Unsatisfactory: Produces work that is often incomplete, incorrect or illegible; demonstrates little evidence of improvement.

EFFICIENCY

Consider ability to prioritize and manage workflow and to make effective use of time and resources.

Outstanding: Develops an orderly personal work routine designed to expedite work flow; experiments with available tools or methods for accomplishing work; adjusts routines to circumstances; views personal job priorities & departmental priorities objectively, making adjustments or suggestions as necessary.

Very Good: Develops an orderly personal work routine designed to expedite work flow; establishes realistic priorities for tasks at hand; makes careful & systematic use of time.

Satisfactory: Develops an orderly personal work routine; establishes realistic priorities for tasks at hand.

Marginal: Develops an inconsistent personal work routine; establishes unrealistic priorities for tasks at hand.

Unsatisfactory: Develops a disorganized personal work routine; does not prioritize tasks at hand.

RELATIONS WITHIN THE DEPARTMENT

Consider willingness to cooperate, ability to get along with others, & ability to communicate. Consider also courtesy, considerateness & helpfulness, & how these factors influence ability to work effectively.

Note: For these purposes, "courteous" means polite; "considerate" means respectful of the rights and feelings of others; and "thoughtful" means that the employee anticipates the wants and needs of others.

WITH CO-WORKERS

Outstanding: Is consistently courteous, considerate, thoughtful & cooperative; willing to assist other staff members; communicates clearly & concisely; initiates action to resolve problems with co-workers; makes suggestions to avoid work problems.

Very Good: Is usually courteous, considerate & cooperative; willing to assist other staff members; communicates clearly & concisely; initiates action to resolve problems.

Satisfactory: Is generally courteous & cooperative; communicates clearly; willing to resolve problems with co-workers.

Marginal: Is sometimes discourteous & inconsiderate; does not initiate resolution to problems with co-workers; sometimes communicates unclearly.

Unsatisfactory: Is often discourteous &/or uncooperative; frequently disrupts work; communicates inappropriately &/or unclearly.

WITH SUBORDINATES

Outstanding: Is courteous, considerate & thoughtful; communicates clearly & concisely; encourages employees to perform independently when possible; assists employees in resolving & avoiding work-related problems; consistently treats employees fairly & without prejudice; encourages employee suggestions to improve departmental performance & implements when possible.

Very Good: Is courteous & considerate; communicates clearly & concisely; allows subordinates to perform without unnecessary interference; assists employees in resolving work-related problems; treats subordinates fairly & without prejudice; accepts employee suggestions to improve departmental performance & implements when possible.

Satisfactory: Is courteous; communicates clearly; allows subordinates to perform with minimal unnecessary interference; is willing to assist employees in resolving work-related problems; usually treats subordinates fairly & without prejudice; is open to employee suggestions to improve departmental performance.

Marginal: Is sometimes discourteous; occasionally communicates unclearly; sometimes unnecessarily interferes with or interrupts subordinates; is not always willing to assist employees in resolving work-related problems; sometimes treats subordinates unfairly or with prejudice; sometimes discourages employee suggestions to improve departmental performance.

Unsatisfactory: Is often discourteous; does not communicate clearly; unnecessarily interferes with or interrupts subordinates; refuses to assist employees in resolving work-related problems; often treats subordinates unfairly or with prejudice; discourages employee suggestions to improve departmental performance.

WITH THE SUPERVISOR

Outstanding: Is consistently courteous, considerate & thoughtful; communicates clearly & concisely; consistently informs supervisor directly of unusual situations; discusses job problems & suggests & implements methods to solve or avoid them; seeks, suggests & implements methods of improving job performance.

Very Good: Is usually courteous & considerate; communicates clearly & concisely; usually informs supervisor directly of unusual situations or problems; discusses job-related problems; seeks & accepts suggestions for improving job performance.

Satisfactory: Is usually courteous; communicates clearly; generally informs supervisor directly of unusual situations or problems; is willing to discuss job-related problems; is open to suggestions for improving job performance.

Marginal: Is sometimes discourteous; occasionally communicates unclearly; does not always inform supervisor directly of unusual situations or problems; resists suggestions for improving performance.

Unsatisfactory: Is often discourteous; does not communicate clearly; does not inform supervisor of unusual situations or problems; rejects suggestions for improving performance.

RELATIONS WITH PERSONNEL FROM OTHER DEPARTMENTS AND/OR THE GENERAL PUBLIC

Take into account the employee's interaction with patrons, employees from other departments and/or general public, either in person or on the telephone. Consider willingness to cooperate and ability to communicate. Consider also tactfulness, courtesy and helpfulness, and how these factors influence ability to work effectively.

Note: For these purposes, "courteous" means polite; "considerate" means respectful of the rights and feelings of others; and "thoughtful" means that the employee anticipates the wants and needs of others.

Outstanding: Assists patrons & other university employees willingly; suggests & implements methods to improve the department's interaction with patrons & other university employees; is consistently courteous, considerate, thoughtful & cooperative; communicates clearly & concisely.

Very Good: Assists patrons & other university employees willingly; is usually courteous, considerate & cooperative; communicates clearly & concisely.

Satisfactory: Is generally courteous & cooperative; usually communicates clearly; assists patrons & other university employees as necessary.

Marginal: Is sometimes discourteous &/or uncooperative; sometimes communicates inappropriately or unclearly; sometimes avoids assisting patrons or other university employees.

Unsatisfactory: Is often discourteous &/or uncooperative with patrons or other university employees; often communicates inappropriately or unclearly; avoids assisting patrons or other university employees.

INITIATIVE

Consider the degree to which the employee is a "self-starter," e.g., able to recognize and effectively follow through on tasks which may not necessarily have been assigned to him/her. The evaluator may also want to consider and measure the extent to which the employee makes an effort to enhance his/her job-related knowledge.

Outstanding: Fulfills job requirements, completing assigned tasks independently; offers ideas & suggestions & helps to implement them; thoroughly investigates all aspects of a problem & limits questions to those which require the supervisor's expertise.

Very Good:	Fulfills job requirements, completing assigned tasks independently; offers ideas & suggestions; consistently & systematically investigates problems before consulting supervisor.
Satisfactory:	Fulfills job requirements, completing assigned tasks independently; makes some effort to investigate solutions to problems before consulting supervisor.
Marginal:	Completes assigned tasks with limited supervision; makes little effort to investigate solutions to problems.
Unsatisfactory:	Does not complete assigned tasks on time; makes no effort to investigate problems; requires considerable supervision while performing tasks.

ADAPTABILITY

Consider ability to handle new or unfamiliar work; to adapt to changes in the work environment and to workflow priorities; and to integrate effectively into the work schedule special assignments.

Outstanding:	Adjusts well & helps to implement changes in work environment; volunteers ideas, time &/or planning skills to facilitate changes & displays great flexibility in implementing special assignments or projects into workflow without disruption of routine.
Very Good:	Adjusts well to changes in work environment; displays flexibility in integrating special assignments or projects into workflow without disruption of routine.
Satisfactory:	Adjusts with little difficulty to changes in work environment; displays flexibility in integrating special assignments or projects into workflow with little disruption of routine.
Marginal:	Has difficulty adjusting to changes in work environment; displays some inflexibility in integrating special assignments or projects into workflow.
Unsatisfactory:	Does not adjust well to changes in work environment; displays inflexibility in integrating special assignments or projects into workflow.

MANAGEMENT SKILLS

Consider effectiveness of both supervisors and non-supervisory personnel who perform these functions.

MANAGEMENT SKILLS: MANAGING WORKFLOW OF OTHERS

Outstanding: Effectively manages the workflow within the unit; resolves workflow problems quickly & effectively; encourages self-sufficiency; delegates responsibility & authority as needed; shows considerable initiative in providing a variety of tasks when appropriate; makes suggestions to increase effective workflow through observation of departmental procedures.

Very Good: Is aware of workflow difficulties & is able to resolve them effectively; is able to manage the workload of employees so that they are always productively occupied; shows initiative in creating & providing a variety of tasks that allow employees to work efficiently & independently.

Satisfactory: Balances the workload and manages the workflow of employees so that they are usually productively occupied; shows some initiative in creating & providing tasks that are beneficial to employees and the unit.

Marginal: Is aware of workflow problems but unsure how to resolve them; has difficulty in balancing workflow of employees; often leaves employees with too much or too little work.

Unsatisfactory: Is unaware of workflow problems affecting employees; is unable to balance workloads; lacks initiative & creativity in originating or providing tasks for employees.

MANAGEMENT SKILLS: SELECTING AND EVALUATING SUBORDINATES

Outstanding: Carefully follows university accepted hiring & evaluation guidelines; monitors staff performance, providing thorough & effective feedback; helps employees set individual & departmental goals; provides encouragement; promotes awareness of job importance; affords opportunities to develop skills.

Very Good: Carefully follows university accepted hiring & evaluation guidelines; monitors staff performance & provides thorough, effective feedback, including helping employees to set individual & departmental goals.

Satisfactory: Follows university accepted hiring & evaluation guidelines; monitors staff performance & provides effective feedback.

Marginal: Displays limited awareness of university accepted hiring & evaluation guidelines; sometimes monitors staff performance & provides inconsistent feedback.

Unsatisfactory: Is unaware of or does not follow university accepted hiring & evaluation guidelines; does not monitor staff performance & does not provide effective feedback.

MANAGEMENT SKILLS: TRAINING ABILITY

Outstanding: Communicates complete job instructions; provides employees with thoroughly updated information; encourages employees to take advantage of opportunities to enrich knowledge; encourages employees' input; provides training according to the needs & abilities of employees.

Very Good: Communicates complete job instructions; provides employees with thoroughly updated information; provides training according to the needs & abilities of employees.

Satisfactory: Communicates basic job instructions; provides employees with adequately updated information.

Marginal: Communicates incomplete job instructions; does not provide employees with adequately updated information.

Unsatisfactory: Does not communicate basic job instructions; does not provide employees with updated information.

MANAGEMENT SKILLS: MAKING DECISIONS, SOLVING PROBLEMS, PROVIDING LEADERSHIP

Outstanding: Sets a conscientious example in work habits; goes to whatever lengths necessary to foresee/define problems & to investigate alternative solutions; makes decisions & always considers impact on others.

Very Good: Sets a consistently good example in work habits; makes a concerted effort to foresee/define problems & to provide workable solutions; makes decisions & usually considers impact on others.

Satisfactory: Sets a good example in work habits; makes some attempt to define problems & find acceptable solutions; makes decisions when necessary.

Marginal: Sets an inconsistent example in work habits; rarely attempts to deal with problems; is reluctant to make decisions.

Unsatisfactory: Sets a poor example in work habits; ignores problems; avoids making decisions.

DEPENDABILITY

Consider reliability, willingness to assume duties of co-workers in their absence, and willingness to give extra time and effort to complete special assignments or important tasks in order to meet departmental goals and obligations.

Outstanding: Volunteers to assume duties of co-workers in their absence to meet departmental needs; always follows through on routine assignments; regards special projects as a challenge & willingly devotes the time & effort necessary to accomplish special assignments.

Very Good: Is willing to assume duties of co-workers in their absence to meet departmental needs; follows through on routine assignments; willing to give time & effort necessary to complete special assignments.

Satisfactory: Is usually willing to assume duties of co-workers in their absence when asked to do so; usually follows through on routine assignments; interested in giving a limited amount of time & effort to complete special assignments.

Marginal: Is reluctant to assume extra duties in the absence of co-workers; rarely follows through on routine assignments; is uninterested in giving extra time & effort to complete special assignments.

Unsatisfactory: Is not willing to assume duties of co-workers in their absence; does not follow through on routine assignments; is not willing to give extra time & effort to complete special assignments.

ATTENDANCE

Outstanding: Within the constraints of the Fair Labor Standards Act, arrives early &/or stays late to accomplish work; plans vacations well ahead of time, taking into consideration the schedule of others & departmental needs; is absent only when necessary; sets the standard for others in adhering to departmental policies concerning attendance & punctuality.

Very Good: Is nearly always on time; is absent only when necessary; keeps supervisor informed of changes in work schedule; maintains appropriate accrued balances of vacation and sick leave to cover scheduled & unexpected absences.

Satisfactory: Is generally on time; is absent only when necessary; usually gives adequate advance notice of absences; does not often run out of leave time to cover excused absences.

Marginal: Has a continuing or sporadic problem with lateness, absenteeism or both which needs correcting and which has a negative impact on workflow & colleagues.

Unsatisfactory: Engages in frequent &/or prolonged absences which have a decidedly negative impact on workflow & other employees &/or repeatedly fails to appear for work at the appointed time &/or fails to call in to report lateness or absences.

CONTRIBUTIONS TO THE MISSION OF THE DEPARTMENT AND THE LIBRARIES IN GENERAL

Consider special projects, committee work (selection, advisory, personnel or any other university or library committees), task forces, publications, community work or any other contributions which enhance the image of the Libraries/Media Systems and the University.

Outstanding: Is committed to several projects/committees outside the general position description &/or assumes extra duties in the absence of the supervisor or other staff members & is able to sustain a superior quality of job performance in the department.

Very Good: Works on projects/committees outside the general position description &/or assumes leadership role in the absence of the supervisor or other staff members & is able to sustain a high quality level of job performance in the department.

SAMPLE OF BEHAVIORALLY
ANCHORED RATING SCALE
Reprinted with
permission of
Iowa City Public Library

IOWA CITY PUBLIC LIBRARY
PERFORMANCE EVALUATION HISTORY

EMPLOYEE NAME:_____

JOB TITLE:_____

DEPARTMENT(S):_____

REPORTING SUPERVISOR:_____

****

CONTENTS:

	JOB DESCRIPTION		ANNUAL GOALS	JOB PERFORMANCE REVIEWS	
	Reviewed	Revised		6 Months	Annual
FY87	_____	_____	_____	_____	_____
FY88	_____	_____	_____	_____	_____
FY89	_____	_____	_____	_____	_____
FY90	_____	_____	_____	_____	_____
FY91	_____	_____	_____	_____	_____
FY92	_____	_____	_____	_____	_____
FY93	_____	_____	_____	_____	_____
FY94	_____	_____	_____	_____	_____
FY95	_____	_____	_____	_____	_____

CONTROL

NA

OBJECTIVE:
Demonstrates control over employees; enforcement of rules and work standards; discipline of employees; evaluation of employees.

Exercises little or no control over employees; fails to enforce rules and work standards; fails to properly discipline employees when necessary; employee evaluations are generally not objective, candid, thorough or substantive, are often based upon subjective criteria and emotional or personal bias, reflect common rating errors, and are frequently submitted late.

In most instances exercises proper control over employees, but occasionally may fail to maintain proper control; sometimes inconsistent in the enforcement of rules and work standards; sometimes reluctant to discipline employees, or is inconsistent in recommending disciplinary measures; employee evaluations are sometimes not objective, candid, thorough or substantive, are sometimes based upon subjective criteria and emotional or personal bias, occasionally reflect common rating errors, but are usually submitted on time.

Generally exercises proper control over employees; generally enforces most rules and work standards properly; generally disciplines employees when necessary in a fair and timely manner; employee evaluations are reasonably objective, candid, thorough and perceptive, with few rating errors and some attention given to providing needed comments and recommendations, and submitted on a timely basis.

Consistently exercises proper control over employees; consistently enforces all rules and work standards; consistently disciplines employees when necessary in a fair and timely manner; employee evaluations are very objective, candid and thorough, clearly depicting the true value of the employee, with no rating errors and proper attention given to providing needed comments and recommendations, and consistently submitted on time.

Always acts with authority and maintains proper control over employees; always enforces all rules and work standards, and sets an excellent example for others; always disciplines employees when necessary in a timely manner, and takes every precaution to assure that the disciplinary measure is fair and consistent; employee evaluations are always unbiased and quite perceptive, showing keen insight into the performance, character and ability of the employee, with no rating errors and extra attention and detail paid to providing needed comments and recommendations, and always submitted on time or ahead of schedule.

SUPERVISOR'S COMMENTS: _____

_____

EMPLOYEE'S RESPONSE: _____

_____

_____

RELATIONS WITH PUBLIC   NA

OBJECTIVE:
Demonstrate courtesy, diplomacy and sincere interest in helping public; ability to answer inquiries properly and give correct information.

Often antagonizes, irritates and argues with public; usually seems insensitive, uncooperative and unresponsive to public; not familiar with Department and thus frequently provides inadequate or incorrect information.	Inconsistent with public; sometimes seems ambivalent and superficial to public; limited familiarity with other Departments and thus sometimes provides inaccurate or incomplete information.	Generally polite and helpful with public; generally seems interested and sincere to public; is familiar with most operations and thus provides correct information or makes appropriate referrals.	Always polite and often makes an extra effort to be helpful to public; always seems concerned and willing to help public; able to provide correct information concerning all routine operations, and follows up when referrals are required.	Always polite and fair to public, and often defuses hostile situations; seems truly concerned, understanding and eager to assist public; consistently provides complete and accurate information on operations, and often takes extra steps to personally obtain such information.

SUPERVISOR'S COMMENTS: _____

EMPLOYEE'S RESPONSE: _____

RELATIONS WITH EMPLOYEES

OBJECTIVE:
Employee contributes to cordial work climate, promotes harmony and enthusiasm and displays sincere interest in assisting and cooperating with other employees.

Frequently rude, disagreeable, resentful and critical of fellow employees; uncooperative and indifferent to employees in other Departments.	Usually courteous but sometimes fails to consider or get along with fellow employees; seldom shows interest in assisting or cooperating with employees in other Departments.	Generally courteous, friendly and considerate of fellow employees and gets along well with them; willing to work and cooperate with employees in other Departments.	Always courteous and friendly with fellow employees and demonstrates tact in dealing with sensitive issues; usually offers to assist and cooperate with employees in other Departments.	Always courteous and friendly with fellow employees, and is available to help others without being asked; goes out of the way to assist employees in other Departments and foster harmonious relations among all employees.

SUPERVISOR'S COMMENTS: _____

EMPLOYEE'S RESPONSE: _____

LEADERSHIP AND SUPERVISION

NA

OBJECTIVE:

Demonstrates good delegation; assignment of employees: effect on employee motivation, teamwork and productivity.

Doesn't delegate or delegates improperly, and frequently fails to match employees to tasks properly; consistently fails to properly or fully utilize employees; unable to motivate employees to develop teamwork, resulting in low productivity.	Delegates properly when directed, but sometimes fails to match employees to tasks properly; sometimes fails to properly or fully utilize employees; sometimes fails to motivate employees or properly develop teamwork, thereby decreasing productivity.	Demonstrates proper skill and understanding in delegating and matching employees to tasks; usually assigns and utilizes employees properly, maintains atmosphere conducive to employee self-motivation, teamwork, and adequate productivity.	Always shows concern and skill in delegating and matching employees to tasks; consistently assigns and utilizes employees properly; implements policies and procedures to encourage self-motivation, teamwork and high productivity.	Consistently shows keen insight in delegating and matching employees to tasks; always makes optimal use of employees; develops and applies policies and procedures to encourage self-motivation, teamwork, and the highest possible productivity.

SUPERVISOR'S COMMENTS:

EMPLOYEE'S RESPONSE:

QUALITY OF WORK

OBJECTIVE:

Skill, competence and knowledge demonstrated by employee; also accuracy, completeness, thoroughness, correctness, preciseness, neatness, carefulness, and workmanship of completed work.

Does not apply job knowledge to tasks; often makes mistakes and errors; and work is consistently sloppy, inaccurate, incomplete and generally unacceptable.	Frequently does not make connection between job knowledge and related tasks; sometimes makes mistakes and errors; and work is sometimes inaccurate, incomplete, imprecise, superficial and only marginally acceptable.	Generally applies job knowledge to assigned tasks; seldom makes mistakes or errors except in complex or unique situations; and work meets general requirements for neatness, accuracy, completeness and precision.	Uses job knowledge to perform tasks efficiently; seldom makes mistakes or errors even in complex or unique situations; and work invariably is outstanding with respect to neatness, accuracy, completeness and precision.	Consistently uses job knowledge to perform tasks and make suggestions for improvements; very seldom makes mistakes or errors; and work consistently excels with respect to neatness, accuracy, completeness and precision.

SUPERVISOR'S COMMENTS: _____

EMPLOYEE'S RESPONSE: _____

QUANTITY OF WORK

OBJECTIVE:

Amount of work generated and successfully completed is compared to amount of work reasonably expected for this job; arrangement and use of time and labor efficiently accomplishes tasks; generally productive.

Never succeeds in completing fair share of work; often wastes time and labor; and is generally very inefficient and nonproductive.	Does not quite meet job requirements; occasionally does not make full use of time and labor; and performs only at a minimally productive level.	Volume of work fully meets job requirements; doesn't waste time or labor; and performs at an acceptable level of productivity.	Volume of work is usually above that normally required for the job; never wastes time or labor; and generally performs at a level of productivity above that normally expected for the job.	Volume of work is consistently far above that normally required for the job; always makes optimum use of time and labor; and always performs at a high level of productivity, while encouraging others to do the same.

SUPERVISOR'S COMMENTS: _____

EMPLOYEE'S RESPONSE: _____

JOB KNOWLEDGE

OBJECTIVE:

Adequate level of knowledge and information is possessed by employee with respect to the job, including technical knowledge, knowledge of duties and responsibilities, and knowledge of policies, codes, laws, rules, procedures, practices and work standards.

Lacks the kinds of knowledge required for satisfactory job performance. Has very little technical knowledge; does not demonstrate knowledge of basic rules and procedures; and does not know what is expected regarding job duties and work standards.	Possesses only limited knowledge necessary for minimal job performance. Has only limited technical knowledge; knows but sometimes overlooks basic rules and procedures; and occasionally must be reminded of job duties and work standards.	Possesses adequate knowledge for good job performance. Has acceptable technical knowledge; knows basic rules and procedures; and demonstrates required knowledge of job duties and work standards.	Work reflects particularly comprehensive and suitable knowledge of the job. Has extensive technical knowledge; knows all basic rules and procedures; and demonstrates consistent knowledge of job duties and work standards.	Exceptionally commanding knowledge of and insight into all aspects of the job. Has expert technical knowledge; understands and can interpret basic and detailed rules and procedures; and assists in outlining job duties and setting work standards.

SUPERVISOR'S COMMENTS: _____

EMPLOYEE'S RESPONSE: _____

JOB APTITUDE AND ATTITUDE

OBJECTIVE:

Is able to understand explanations, follow directions, learn procedures, accept responsibility, and adapt to new routines and situations.

Repeatedly needs detailed instructions and misunderstands instructions; unable to follow routine procedures; unable to accept responsibility; resists change and is upset by new approaches.	Requires considerable instructions; has some difficulty following routine procedures; reluctant sometimes to accept responsibility; and has difficulty in adjusting to changes or new approaches.	Understands and is able to follow instructions; satisfactorily performs routine procedures; accepts and acknowledges responsibility; accepts changes, new approaches, new ideas and works well with them.	Requires only general instructions; consistently performs routine procedures; displays well above average sense of responsibility; receptive to changes, new approaches, new ideas, and applies them effectively.	Requires only minimal instructions; performs both routine and complex procedures; accepts full responsibility for himself/herself and assigned subordinates, and often requests greater responsibility; immediately grasps and often suggests improvements, new approaches, new ideas

SUPERVISOR'S COMMENTS: _____

EMPLOYEE'S RESPONSE: _____

DEPENDABILITY

OBJECTIVE:

Demonstrates reliability and willingness to accept responsibility; degree of supervision required; ability to follow work schedules and meet deadlines; production of work under pressure.

Not very reliable; requires constant close supervision; is consistenly behind schedule and seldom meets deadlines; seems overwhelmed by common problems and frequently requires assistance.	Reasonably conscientious and usually reliable; requires more than usual amount of supervision; is occasionally behind schedule and sometimes misses deadlines; handles routine work well, but sometimes unable to handle emergencies effectively.	Conscientious and reliable; requires only general supervision in routine matters; generally complies with work schedules and meets deadlines; capably handles routine work and generally responds well in emergencies.	Conscientious and very reliable; requires little supervision even for non-routine matters; consistently complies with work schedules and meets deadlines; very capable in handling both routine and emergency situations.	Dedicated and totally reliable; requires no supervision; regardless of inconvenience, invariably meets most difficult commitments and deadlines, often ahead of schedule, always handles routine work in a professional manner, and assumes leadership in handling emergency situations.

SUPERVISOR'S COMMENTS:

_____

_____

EMPLOYEE'S RESPONSE:

_____

_____

USE OF TOOLS, EQUIPMENT, AND FACILITIES

DEFINITION:

Safe and skillful operation of proper tools, equipment. Care and maintenance of tools, equipment, and facilities.

Frequently uses wrong tools and equipment; lacks needed skills in operation of tools and equipment and frequently uses them improperly; often violates safety rules and endangers self and others; abuses tools, equipment; fails to report needed repairs and ignores maintenance requirements.	Sometimes uses wrong tools and equipment; demonstrates skills in use of tools and equipment to minimally perform the job and seldom uses them improperly; very seldom forgets safety rules; on occasion improperly cares for tools and equipment, and sometimes needs to be reminded of maintenance requirements.	Generally uses proper tools and equipment; demonstrates skillful use of tools and equipment to adequately perform the job and never knowingly uses them improperly; never consciously disregards safety rules; generally uses tools and equipment in a careful manner; and sees that proper maintenance is performed.	Always uses proper tools and equipment; usually demonstrates high level of skill in use of tools and equipment and never uses them improperly; never disregards safety rules; always uses tools and equipment in a careful manner; and assures that needed repairs are made and proper maintenance is performed.	NA

SUPERVISOR'S COMMENTS:

_____

_____

EMPLOYEE'S RESPONSE:

_____

_____

PLANNING, ORGANIZING, AND COORDINATING   NA

OBJECTIVE:
Demonstrates ability in planning and organizing to achieve goals; scheduling and coordinating work (among employees and with other Divisions).

Frequently fails to plan or organize work properly; does not schedule work properly and shows little coordination among the employees of other Divisions.	Sometimes fails to plan or organize work well; efforts at scheduling work are inconsistent.	Plans and organizes work well; generally schedules work and coordinates activities to avoid duplication and provide necessary support from other employees or Divisions.	Consistently plans and organizes work well; always schedules work properly and coordinates activities among all employees and Divisions involved.	Consistently plans and organizes work in an effective and innovative manner; always schedules work properly and demonstrates leadership in coordinating activities among all employees and Divisions involved; consistently shows keen insight in delegating and matching employees to tasks.

SUPERVISOR'S COMMENTS:

EMPLOYEE'S RESPONSE:

DECISION MAKING AND JUDGEMENT   NA

OBJECTIVE:
Appropriate use of judgement in making decisions; soundness and timeliness of decisions; analytical ability.

Unreliable judgement, overlooks pertinent considerations and has little sense of proportion; puts off making decisions and often makes poor decisions; analysis of facts, data and policies frequently incomplete and lacking in thoroughness and accuracy.	Judgement adequate if clear-cut precedents exist, but lacks practicality, wisdom and sensitivity in new situations; sometimes slow in making decisions unless pushed, and occasionally jumps too hastily to conclusions; tends to accept statements or events with little critical thought, and sometimes fails to interpret or analyze facts and data adequately.	Exercises good judgement in dealing with all normal situations and most unusual situations; generally makes sound decisions with reasonable promptness; generally identifies the facts or underlying events, ideas or problems, and interprets and analyzes them with reasonable accuracy.	Consistently exercises good judgement in all types of situations, and always carefully considers all facts and possible courses of action, as time permits; always makes sound decisions in a very timely and confident manner; successfully examines the essential elements of problem situations, analysis of facts, data and policies are complete, thorough and accurate.	Displays excellent judgement, timing and insight even in the most difficult and sensitive situations, and judgement is unimpaired by work pressures; consistently makes excellent decisions with outstanding speed and success, even when under acute pressure; exceptionally effective in reaching the heart of a difficult problem, evaluating its elements, and their significance, and making an extremely accurate and thorough analysis.

SUPERVISOR'S COMMENTS:

EMPLOYEE'S RESPONSE:

COMMUNICATION SKILLS

OBJECTIVE: Demonstrates ability to receive, process and communicate information, including the ability to prepare and present written and oral reports which are clear, accurate and complete.

Frequently fails to understand or communicate information accurately to others; and unable to speak or write clearly as required by the job.	Sometimes has difficulty understanding or communicating information accurately to others. If appropriate, can prepare simple written reports and oral presentations, but they sometimes require revision or improvement.	Understand oral and written information and accurately communicates it to others; written reports and oral presentations are complete, properly organized, well understood and rarely require change.	Understands all oral and written information, often clarifies it, and always makes sure others understand it; written reports and oral presentations are well prepared, effective and quite convincing; proper diction and good projection.	Fully understands all oral and written information, is able to properly analyze and interpret it, and convey it with proper connotations to stress intent and importance; written reports and oral presentations always reflect the utmost qualities of clarity, accuracy, precision, organization, and persuasiveness; proper diction and excellent projection

SUPERVISOR'S COMMENTS: _____

EMPLOYEE'S RESPONSE: _____

INITIATIVE AND RESOURCEFULLNESS

OBJECTIVE: Demonstrates self-motivation and self-reliance; desire to do better and find new improved methods and procedures; willingness to do more than required; and level of resourcefulness in performing job duties and responsibilities.

Constantly has to be told and reminded what and how to do things, and relies heavily on others; never suggests improvements or new ideas; shows no imagination or resourcefulness.	Slow in getting started, must have instructions, and sometimes must be reminded to keep busy; seldom suggests new or better ways to do things; usually goes strictly "by the book," but sometimes displays originality.	Performs routine work generally without requiring instructions, and usually stays busy; occasionally suggests new or better ways to do things; displays imagination, originality and resourcefulness.	Grasps situations and goes to work without hesitation, seldom requires instruction, and always stays busy; often suggests new or better ways to do things; shows resourcefulness in dealing with difficult problems.	A self-starter who anticipates and plans own work, always busy, and encourages others to think and work; analyzes problems and frequently suggests new methods, procedures and techniques; highly adept in applying imagination and resourcefulness to difficult problems.

SUPERVISOR'S COMMENTS: _____

EMPLOYEE'S RESPONSE: _____

IOWA CITY PUBLIC LIBRARY PERFORMANCE APPRAISAL

FY _____ REVIEW SHEET FOR _____

SEMI ANNUAL _____

ANNUAL _____

INSTRUCTIONS

1. JOB DESCRIPTION: Review for accuracy. Document changes agreed upon. Comment, at the minimum, on all job responsibilities where employee surpasses or fails to meet standards and/or procedures.

2. ANNUAL GOALS: Make a comment upon each FY goal. Accomplished? Skillfully? Drop? Continue? Add to job description? Draft goals for next FY. Agree on deadline or other method of measurement. Attach draft copy to this sheet.

3. OTHER PERTINENT ITEMS: List any topics discussed. Document any action taken by employee or supervisor. If pink form is used, attach to this sheet. Factors that may result in denial of merit must be noted.

4. SEMI-ANNUAL: May do all of the above or may simply follow instructions in #3.

SUPERVISOR'S REMARKS

SIGNATURE _____ DATE _____

EMPLOYEE'S REMARKS

SIGNATURE _____ DATE _____

INDEX